The
Magdalene
Gospel

THE
MAGDALENE
GOSPEL

MARY ELLEN ASHCROFT

DOUBLEDAY
NEW YORK LONDON TORONTO SYDNEY AUCKLAND

PUBLISHED BY DOUBLEDAY
a division of Bantam Doubleday Dell Publishing Group, Inc.
1540 Broadway, New York, New York 10036

DOUBLEDAY and the portrayal of an anchor with a dolphin
are trademarks of Doubleday, a division of Bantam
Doubleday Dell Publishing Group, Inc.

The Scripture quotations contained herein are from the New Revised
Standard Version Bible, copyright © 1989 by the Division of Christian
Education of the National Council of the Churches of Christ in the
U.S.A. Used by permission. All rights reserved.

Book design by Jennifer Ann Daddio
Illustrations by Kate Brennan Hall

Library of Congress Cataloging-in-Publication Data
Ashcroft, Mary Ellen, 1952–
    The Magdalene gospel / Mary Ellen Ashcroft. — 1st ed.
        p.   cm.
    1. Mary Magdalene, Saint—Fiction.   2. Bible. N.T.—
History of Biblical events—Fiction.   3. Christian women
saints—Palestine—Fiction.   4. Women in the Bible—
Fiction.   5. Jesus Christ—Fiction.
PS3551.S367M33   1995
813'.54—dc20   95-3026
                                                        CIP

ISBN 0-385-47855-0

10   9   8   7   6   5   4

For worship is the submission of all our nature to God. It is the quickening of conscience by His holiness; the nourishment of mind with His truth; the purifying of imagination by His beauty; the opening of the heart to His love; the surrender of will to His purpose—and all of this gathered up in adoration, the most selfless emotion of which our nature is capable.

—WILLIAM TEMPLE, *Readings in St. John's Gospel,* 67

For Letha, who has been for me what the women in The Magdalene Gospel *are for each other, a source of inexhaustible friendship and a constant challenge to grow in my faith and worship.*

ACKNOWLEDGMENTS

My special thanks to my husband Ernie for his constant support and to my children Andrew, Stephen, and Susannah for their consistent "Go for it, Mom!" attitude.

My friends Barb Olson, Mary Schneekloth, Laura Jensen, Dan Taylor, Jan Lindholm, Lori Goetz, Chris Tachick, and Letha Wilson-Barnard read drafts, never failing to offer good advice and encouragement. Special encouragement came from Peg Thompson, Richard Bierman, Holly Elliott, Kent and Stephanie Nelson, and Jill Wright.

Jo Bailey-Wells, who acted as chauffeur, guardian angel, and guide during my trip to Israel, also deserves great appreciation.

Thanks to Judy Hornbacher, Janelle Colley, Letha Wilson-Barnard, Barb Olson, Kathy Nevins, and Shelley Potter for giving voice to the different women in *The Magdalene Gospel* at a reading.

Segments of this work in progress were presented at women's retreats at St. Stephen's and Messiah Episcopal churches as well as the Minnesota Diocesan Convention, Salem Covenant, and Christ Presbyterian churches.

Thanks to Doubleday editor, Mark Fretz, for his helpful comments and input on the manuscript.

Finally, I must express my appreciation for the support and love of my two house groups—the one at Messiah where this project started, and the one at St. Stephen's, which supports me now.

Now when he rose early on the first day of the week, [Jesus] appeared first to Mary Magdalene, from whom he had cast out seven demons. She went out and told those who had been with him, while they were mourning and weeping. But when they heard that he was alive and had been seen by her, they would not believe it.

—MARK 16:9–11

Mary Magdalene has a story to tell. In the gospels of Matthew, Mark, Luke, and John she is identified as a woman healed by Jesus. According to the four canonical stories she becomes a close follower of Jesus, a witness of his crucifixion, and one of the first to see and talk to the risen Jesus. This is what the gospel writers tell us about the young Magdalene woman.

In Luke 8, we meet Mary as she encounters Jesus for the first time. Ever after, her story is intertwined with his. She follows Jesus wandering throughout Palestine, eventually to the cross, and finally greets him at the tomb on Easter morning. Yet, after Jesus ascends into heaven, Mary remains. She continues following Jesus. In time Mary Magdalene's story becomes part of the good news about Jesus.

There seems to be more to this woman who chose to follow Jesus than what we hear and see in the gospels.

Especially when the stories focus on the climactic death and resurrection of Jesus, Mary unexpectedly attracts a good share of attention. She must have more to say; but despite our piqued interest, the gospels do not tell *her* story. For whatever reason, as with all the women who encounter and follow Jesus, she never gets to tell her own story. Her voice and the voices of women disciples as a whole become muffled whispers in the gospels. Like the soothing sound of a mother humming softly to her suckling child, these women's voices, though quiet, offer warmth, healing, and love, as Jesus had done for them.

Mary Magdalene experienced Jesus as a woman. Her story is the Good News (gospel) of a woman—*The Magdalene Gospel*. Like Mary, many women followed Jesus: his mother, women he healed or whose children he made well, women he befriended, women who found new life in him. They are unique individuals, who for the most part are lumped into the category of "the women." These women share many traits in common, most notably their capacity to care for others as Jesus cared for them. But, each has a special story to tell of her life and her relationship to Jesus.

The Magdalene Gospel is an imaginative retelling of the gospel narratives from the perspective of Jesus' women followers, a new way to hear the good news. It sheds new light on the gospels and offers a new way to see Jesus. It gives voice to these women, so close to Christ, who've been silenced for centuries. It offers both their individual stories—as each was touched by Jesus—and their common story. Together after the death of their friend and teacher on that first Holy Saturday, they are doing for each other what women do—supporting and comforting—as they try to make sense of his life and his death.

The Magdalene Gospel began with a challenge from a friend. Why, Scott asked, aren't you writing about the gospels from a woman's perspective? I had the background: some seminary classes, years in the Anglican church in England, South Africa, and the United States. I'd done graduate work on issues of women's discourse and written a book looking at sin and temptation from a woman's perspective—Temptations Women Face (InterVarsity Press, 1991).

I was leaving on a two-month trip, and Scott's challenge stuck. With time to immerse myself in the gospels, I began seeing them through the eyes of the women disciples. Mary Magdalene captured my attention. What would it have been like to be this woman whose life was overturned by her encounter with Christ? I wrote pages traveling with Jesus, watching him through her eyes, listening to his words. And Mary Magdalene introduced me to other women disciples. What would it have been like to be the woman with the hemorrhage of blood, hopeless before she crept to touch Jesus? Or the twisted woman in Luke 13, unable to look up for eighteen years, until she looked into the face of the teacher? Deeply moved, I felt I was beginning to see Jesus through new lenses and to hear the gospel proclaimed in a new voice.

I realized that I needed to move out of the gospels and into the library. The power in the women's individual stories was magnified as I saw the gospel accounts of Jesus' action contrasted with historical accounts of contemporary cultural norms. I read about the restrictions on a woman who had a discharge of blood; I discovered that Jesus made a remarkable statement in Luke 13 when he called the newly upright woman "a daughter of Abraham," as no rabbi had called a woman before.

The women were there as their teacher was being killed. I began to realize how extraordinary it was that a number of women followers had undertaken the week-long journey (without husbands or fathers) to stand with their rabbi. Why, I wondered, have I never heard this before? Of all the sermons I've listened to, none touched on this startling element of the story. How in the world, when Jesus' ministry with women expected their theological reflection, demanded their discipleship—against all cultural norms of the time—how can "biblical scholars" get away with endless interpretations of verses about headship in Ephesians or I Corinthians or whether women can pray (in I Timothy), conveniently ignoring the life and actions of the one they claim to follow?

Before long, I had notebooks bulging with women's stories, pages of historic data, notes from travel to Galilee and Jerusalem. One day, re-reading the passion story in Luke, I realized that the women were together, that "The women who had come with him from Galilee followed, and they saw the tomb and how his body was laid. Then they returned, and prepared spices and ointments. On the sabbath they rested according to the commandment." (Luke 23:55–56). *The Magdalene Gospel* takes place at Bethany on that Sabbath. On one level, this book is a product of my imagination, based on the gospel accounts; on another level it is what I believe might well have happened, what probably happened on that first day after Jesus' death.

Mary Magdalene is central to this gospel, not only because she was the first witness to the resurrection (in an era where women's evidence was not admissable in a court of law), but because I recognized in her a remarkable range of understanding and emotion. These make her the Everywoman of this account. Mary Magdalene loses herself completely, and needs to be called back to herself by Christ. As *The Magdalene Gospel* opens, she has lost herself again, and needs to be called back by reliving the healing work of God as well as by hearing the voices of her sister disciples. She is drawn, on that first Holy Saturday, from a simple message of divine deliverance to a message more difficult than she'd dreamed. Only then can she find Christ again.

The women gathered that Sabbath to tell their stories. You can join them. As you read about their lives, enter into each individual story. Experience the reality of their encounters with Jesus by using your five senses. Pause between stories or sections and imagine sharing your own story in this circle of women. Reflect on the depth of feelings and contemplate the new dimensions of the gospel stories never considered before hearing *The Magdalene Gospel*.

You may begin studying the gospels from the perspective of Mary Magdalene and her companions. For your study of the Bible, I have listed the biblical passages (see Endnotes) on which the stories are based. I have also listed a few of the historical details that seem most relevant to their stories.

I have used much of the material in *The Magdalene Gospel* for retreats and presentations. You may find them suitable as the basis of sermons and meditations, or as a study group resource. Groups benefit from having a reader or actor dramatically read one of the stories (for instance, the woman with the hemorrhage of blood or Martha's story). Allow some time for silence. You could then pose questions for the group to ponder quietly, reflect on in writing, or discuss.

This is a sampling of the ways you might join the circle and enter into the story-telling.

Mary Magdalene's gospel is not frivolous, superficial "good news." Woven with the words of her gathered sisters, it is the good news which shows light even in darkness. Their good news pulls us back from the nightmare edge and gives us hope and purpose in a community of faith.

ONE

PROLOGUE

Then Jesus, crying with a loud voice, said, "Father, into your hands I commend my spirit." Having said this, he breathed his last. When the centurion saw what had taken place, he praised God and said, "Certainly this man was innocent." And when all the crowds who had gathered there for this spectacle saw what had taken place, they returned home, beating their breasts. **But all his acquaintances, including the women who had followed him from Galilee, stood at a distance, watching these things.**

Now there was a good and righteous man named Joseph, who, though a member of the council, had not agreed to their plan and action. He came from the Jewish town of Arimathea, and he was waiting expectantly for the kingdom of God. This man went to Pilate and asked for the body of Jesus. Then he took it down, wrapped it in a linen cloth, and laid it in a rock-hewn tomb where no one had ever been laid. **It was the day of Preparation, and the sabbath was beginning. The women who had come with him from Galilee followed, and they saw the tomb and how his body was laid. Then they returned, and prepared spices and ointments. On the sabbath they rested according to the commandment.**

—LUKE 23:46–56

How does she feel as she gropes toward waking on that Sabbath?

Mary Magdalene has hurled herself at life. The most preco-cious child in her village—always scrupulous in keeping the law, wild to please her father, desperate to placate God. Craving love, the most adventurous in exploring her sexuality. Then the steep drop-off as she plunged in over her head, in past remembering.

People talk about being in shock, about physical symptoms associated with loss. But they forget the crescendos and the pianis-simos of one like Mary Magdalene, for whom each tremor of fear is an earthquake, each thrill of spiritual understanding a vision. Dazzling light and suffocating blackness have crisscrossed her life with horror and wonder. This morning the darkness crushes her.

Blackness. That's all there is for Mary Magdalene this Sab-bath. A few days before she had been squinting for a light at the end of the tunnel, but a landslide has crashed down, blocking the way ahead. All she can do is tear at the walls and struggle for breath.

But no. There is one faint glimmer, one breath of fresh air. As she wakes from her nightmares, she realizes that she is not alone.

On this first Holy Saturday the women who traveled with Jesus from Galilee and who followed him in Jerusalem are drawn together. They comfort one another and defy the darkness all that day and through the night. From one another, they draw strength and begin their struggle to understand Jesus' life and death.

Less than twenty-four hours after his death, these women make the day sacred by their faith and love.

As she struggles from her fitful sleep, Mary Magdalene feels that she is being pulled backward—sucked into nightmares of murky despair, helpless possession. Had she been alone—who knows what might have happened? She needs them, desperately, to wrest her from the void, to help her battle the goblins of her night terrors, this morning after his death.

A navy-violet sky, a full moon hangs ominously over the tombs. She walks through the Kidron valley, caves, no . . . graves loom left and right. A black pit, a newly-dug tomb. Fear begins to choke her; strange—it is not fear for herself. Her friend, her teacher—it is for him that she trembles.

"Don't be afraid." That's what he said, over and over. "Don't be afraid." But the rising panic washes over her litany like a wave, silencing her voice.

He must be afraid. He must be terrified.

Her legs—young and vigorous only yesterday—refuse to run. He is ahead; he's gone past the tombs. The graves spell death, his death.

She must find him. Only she can comfort him in his terror. "Rabbouni, I will wait with you. I will watch with you. . . ." She shouts, but her cry is lost, swept into empty tombs and gone. This time her voice rises to a shriek: "I will be with you and watch and wait. Rabbouni . . ."

The women move to her. Caring for a sick child, watching with a woman in labor, sitting with a dying neighbor: they are not afraid to touch her, to weep with her. She drags her heavy head back and forth across the mat as she wakens. A dream . . . oh my God . . . her terror begins to recede. But the blessed emptiness is

swept aside by utter despair and dread, crashing over her like a breaker. He is not alone. He is not afraid. He is dead.

The mallet, driving the stake through his wrist, pounds through her temples. His dripping blood seems to seep from her own eyes and nose. Jeers and raucous laughter echo in her head. She pulls her hand across her eyes, trying to wipe the blood . . . blood dripping in his eyes. Flies stuck to his face.

She pulls her head across the mat, her groan echoing his cry —his scream of desolation. It will never stop reverberating through her consciousness. The cross tips up again and thumps into the ground, tearing his flesh. Time will always be stuck there, his death played over and over.

The murmur of their voices and their touch pull her back from the edge of the abyss.

"Mary, Mary. We're here."

"It is so hard. . . ."

"What was she before he freed her?"

"Her whole life . . . following him, loving him."

Mary Magdalene's long dark hair covers her face. Her dirty blue tunic is twisted around her legs. She pulls herself to a sitting position and begins to push her tangled hair off her tear-soaked face. The sun is skirting a cloud and its patterns ripple on the straw mat. She stares around at the faces, unraveling them from the

shadows of her mind. From face to face, she finds it is like looking in a mirror, but one that looks back at her with familiarity and warmth.

Their faces wet with tears and drawn by pain: who are these women who sit with Mary Magdalene?[1] Salome who was with her at the tomb. Joanna, Rhoda and Lydia—they had journeyed from Galilee to Jerusalem with Jesus—only ten days ago? Susannah— who was as a mother to her in Capernaum—and also traveled with them. In the corner, Miriam, also known as Mary Clopas, who was at the tomb. She holds the hand of Jesus' mother, white and fragile, staring. Martha and her sister Maria whose hospitality they share.

The women sit on mats on the floor, together, but they do not know each other well. The Galilean followers are as sisters, of course, from their years of following the teacher. Martha and Maria, who have come to know Jesus from his visits to the city during the great festivals, have met the Galilean women briefly before. Although all the women wear similar tunics and head coverings, they must concentrate to understand each other's accents; they stumble over little variations in customs and manners. Neither their clothing nor their manners indicate what may be their deepest disparity, that of religious sensibility, since the Jerusalem disciples have centered their faith on temple worship, and the country women on the Torah and the synagogue.

But this morning the women have woken together. Thrown together in their love, in their astounding new lives. And now together in their devastating loss.

Martha kneels beside Mary Magdalene holding out a pottery bowl.

"Drink this. It's hot."

She sips the bitter liquid, then takes the bowl and drinks deeply.

The house is chilly this early spring morning. And although no one can light a fire on the Sabbath, Martha has thought to keep one over from the day before, and to keep some water hot over-night.[2]

What would they talk about—these women who had lost their life's blood?

Mary Magdalene stares at the empty bowl. Salome, her dark curly hair speckled with white, speaks, as if she were in the middle of a sentence when Mary awoke. Like people who have survived a terrible accident or a near fatal illness, she needs to tell her story. Over and over, these women will need to speak about what has happened. This is the first time, and Salome's voice seems loud in the room.

We knew Jesus was dead. Then we heard the soldiers talking. Saying how one of the sympathizers on the council had asked Pilate for permission to bury Jesus, but they couldn't let him have the body till they were sure he was dead. Joseph—we figured he was the sympathizer—arrived and stood next to us. The soldiers went to the other crosses and broke their legs. They were moving toward Jesus . . .

"Jesus is dead," I said to Joseph, and he started to explain that with the Sabbath coming and the festival, it was the soldiers' job to make sure they all suffocated. I was arguing with him and the other soldier . . . slashed open Jesus' side. They took him down.

It is difficult for the women to look at each other while this story is being told. Pain fills the room, but it is hardest to look at Jesus' mother. Salome speaks again.

Joseph and another man—a teacher I think—moved the body to where we were standing. We held him. I looked at him, there in my arms, and couldn't believe he was dead. Joseph said time was running short and if we wanted to get Jesus' body in a safe, respectable place before the Sabbath started, we needed to get moving. . . . We wrapped him in a linen cloth. . . .[3]

All the women were at the cross, but only a few at the tomb —Mary Magdalene, Salome and Miriam.[4] With a glance at these bewildered women, it is not hard to understand why. The Friday was not only excruciating, it was dangerous. All of Jesus' followers would have known that friends or family seen mourning at a crucifixion might themselves be crucified. Martha and Maria had taken Jesus' mother home, along with several of the other older women who had stayed at the cross until he was dead.

Jesus' mother and the others want desperately to picture him free from pain, to think of that torn body resting quietly some-where.

Miriam holds Jesus' mother and speaks to her.

Mary, you were there when he died.

Living in neighboring villages, they have known each other so long that they are like sisters. She turns to the others.

She grieves that she came home before she saw him laid in the tomb. I've told her, over and over, that I was there, watching with her eyes. . . . And she and Joanna and Lydia got some of the spices and ointments mixed up before the Sabbath began.

Pulling Jesus' mother's head onto her shoulder, she speaks to her again.

You needed to come home. He was dead. He didn't know you weren't there. And what if we'd been seen at the tomb?

It was the most beautiful linen cloth that they wrapped him in.

Salome wants to finish the story, because telling it eases her pain:

Joseph asked where we were spending the Sabbath. We told him we'd be here in Bethany. He said we should probably get moving if we wanted to get over the hill before sunset.

We looked at each other and knew we weren't leaving until we had seen exactly where they put Jesus. The Romans would torture people in a garbage dump.

Miriam interrupts Salome, hoping to quiet Mary's dread:

But the place where they took his body was a garden, my dear, and a nicer spot you couldn't expect to find. And they carefully put his body in a clean, fresh tomb, and we went in and looked at him, and touched him, and then Joseph said he wanted to get it closed up, so we kissed Jesus one last time.

A silence hangs over the women. Then Mary Magdalene doubles over, sobbing, her mind chilled with the dank stone walls, the cold of his body. She struggles to her feet, crying that she needs to be with him. The others want to calm Mary, but they are torn by their own feelings. This is Martha and Maria's home, their city. The sisters speak.

Mary. Have another hot drink.

You cannot go to him now—none of us can. This isn't Galilee.

We will go early, first thing tomorrow and take ointments and give him the sort of burial he deserves.

It is the Sabbath. We must wait.

Mary Magdalene rocks back and forth on her knees, sobbing.

Alone, alone. And all those last hours he was alone.

The darkness of the garden overpowers her.

I can't bear it. There by the cross. John. He stared at Jesus and told me that when Jesus was praying in the garden . . . they didn't understand . . . Jesus needed someone to comfort him . . . to tell him not to be afraid. They . . . fell asleep.

Judas gone to the Sanhedrin . . . Jesus knew. . . . He walked down through Kidron . . . those mouths shouting death to him.

And then in that garden. The light of the moon, playing in the olive trees. Jesus trying to pray. Trying to block his ears to the sound of his killers' coming.

All alone. John and the others asleep. Jesus could have bolted—up over the hill . . . into the desert. He'd be alive. . . . Not cold and alone in that tomb . . .

Her voice has become almost a shout. Now it drops to a whisper.

What wouldn't I give to have been with him in the garden? I would have sat with him, prayed with him, held him. . . . He was wretched, only terror as his companion. He knew what was coming. . . .

Mary Magdalene covers her face with her hands, sobbing. They all stare, contemplating his dread in the garden, remembering his hours of torture on the cross.

As the silence stretches into minutes, another fear creeps into the room. It sidles up to each woman, suggesting that the joy has been an empty dream, whispering that she will soon forget her new life.

Who might have first spoken this fear? Lydia, the tall, slender woman sitting near Mary Magdalene, begins to weep.

I am so frightened . . . that I will forget. For almost two years my life has been illumined by the light of God. Now it has been extinguished. What if I forget what light is like?

The women murmur their agreement. Joanna, who sits next to Lydia nods.

When my son died, I promised myself I would never forget him. But now I hardly remember his face, his smile, his hand in mine. And when I think I remember, I wonder if my memory is playing tricks on me. If he passed me in the market, would I know him?

For the first time, Jesus' mother stirs.

From his first quickening within me, I have known him. But perhaps even I will forget.

Miriam holds her hand.

Yesterday in the tomb, I looked at him as closely as I could. For myself and for you, his own mother. I tried to etch in my mind every detail of his face. I don't want us to forget how he looked, what he did, what he said. . . .

There is strength in the closeness of these women. But who is the first to realize her riches, even in her loss? Martha puts down a jug of steaming liquid, and kneels by Lydia, stroking her head.

We will not forget. Don't you see? We have . . . our stories. You walked with Jesus in Galilee, but that part of his life is hidden to Maria and me. We remember other days and teachings.

She speaks to her sister, as one who is trying to convince herself.

We will not allow each other to forget. We won't, Maria. . . .

Maria looks around the women's faces as they all stare at her. She shakes her head.

No. We will not forget.

Martha stands, pushing back her hair, and then squats to face Lydia.

Please. Tell us how you met him.

Lydia bows her head slightly. She has a dignity, almost an awkwardness, built on years of isolation and humiliation.
In the scriptures she is given no name; if she's mentioned, it is as the woman with a hemorrhage of blood, an interruption in the story about the raising of Jairus' daughter.
It's hard for a contemporary woman to imagine what each

woman in this circle knew as a monthly reality: seven days treated as if she were filthy and contagious. But for Lydia—suffering from a vaginal discharge meant that she was always unclean, that anyone who touched her, who sat where she sat or lay where she had lain, was unclean.[5]

It is difficult to look at Lydia without being aware of the deep inner strength of one who has traveled to the depths of human despair, and found (unexpectedly) that there is hope.[6]

She begins her story.

I grew up in Capernaum. My parents died when I was a child, and because of my illness I could never marry.

For twelve years I suffered from a hemorrhage of blood. Most days I was weak, dizzy, and wracked by pain. Year in, year out, I sought help. I saw healers and doctors, tried the home remedy suggested by my neighbor's aunt, the crushed roots recommended by the woman who lived behind me. I journeyed time and again to other towns in Galilee where there was a doctor that I hadn't seen, a healer I heard rumors of. Often I would get up before dawn and travel beyond my strength—perhaps five or six hours of walking—and then wait. I was careful to stay away from the other patients, but if they heard that a woman was there with a discharge, they would mumble, stare, scold their children to stay away from me.

Many times, the sun rose up to its height and then started to sink toward the horizon. Others who came after me were called. Sometimes when I was finally brought in to see the doctor, he would not examine me. He had other appointments and demands; it would be inconvenient for him to be made unclean by me. I was unmarried; I couldn't have children. Why should a doctor make himself unclean to try to make me well? I thought of coming to Jerusalem to consult a doctor, but the journey was too long for my weakened body. And how could I have come to the holy city, but not go into the temple, because of my uncleanness?

After twelve years, my money was gone and I was weaker and sicker and more lonely than ever before. My years of usefulness as a woman had trickled away from me, like sands in an hourglass . . . gone . . . gone. . . .

I came to believe God was against me. Because of the law of Moses, I could never touch or be touched by a man. I couldn't enter a neighbor's house without making it unclean. I could not have guests come to a meal because the food I prepared was unclean. All the restrictions that you my sisters have once a moon, I knew as my life's reality. I could never go to worship—Sabbath after Sabbath I heard the children on their way to synagogue, the parents, talking quietly.

I began to feel that I was Eve—the gateway of destruction as the teachers in the village call her. I wondered if all that men have said of us is true—that women lead to filth and degradation. I felt like a soiled rag. I began to want more than anything to go to sleep and never wake again. My life was reeling by in a haze of weakness, pain, and despair.

Then I heard about a new rabbi in Capernaum. Rumors flew that he was a miracle worker. Maybe . . .

maybe . . . I let myself think, maybe, this new rabbi will be the answer. I dared to allow myself to imagine—just for a moment—a life of health, wholeness, friends. . . .

Then I remembered. Fool! I said to myself. He would never touch you . . . he would become unclean. Maybe he would lose his special powers.

But I overheard someone saying that he touched lepers. Maybe . . . for days I tried to figure out how to get close to him, how to touch him without his knowing, without his followers sending me away, telling me to take my unclean self away from their holy master.

He's a miracle man; perhaps he would know I was nearby and shout, "Don't touch me! Take this filthy woman away before she touches me!"

Even if you got near him, I told myself, his touch probably wouldn't work. But I also told myself I had nothing to lose. This would be my last chance.

I must try. That next day . . . I knew he was in the village . . . I would try to sneak close and touch him.

I got up early, my stomach knotted with fear. I felt weaker and dizzier than usual . . . maybe, I thought, I should wait until tomorrow and see if I felt better . . . no, I knew it had to be today . . . I dressed and tried to eat.

Then I moved toward the village center listening for the sound of a crowd. Yes, I heard them, a large group surrounding Jesus. He had stopped. I leaned this way and that, keeping my veil over my face, but trying to see who was kneeling in front of Jesus.

No, no. It was a ruler of the synagogue. He knew who I was . . . he was nearly sobbing, telling Jesus that his only daughter was dying, pleading with Jesus to come and heal her. Jesus nodded and began to follow the ruler. Surrounded by the crowd, they moved in my direction.

I started to step forward, the crowd noise dimming in my ears. How could I touch Jesus now? How could I make him unclean at a time like this? A ruler of the synagogue is an important man, and he has prominent friends. It is a child who is sick or perhaps dead. What kind of woman would make Jesus unclean at a time like this?

Perhaps, I told myself, if I just brushed against him, just touched the fringe at the bottom of his robe. Maybe just a tiny bit of his power, just enough to heal me and he'd never know and the crowd would never know and he could go on his important business. . . .

I moved nearer and nearer in the crowd. He was a few people away and then just one person away, and then I was next to him. I moved behind him and bent down as if I'd dropped something. I touched the fringe on his robe.

That moment, my sisters, stretched out forever. I felt warmth move up my arm and through my body and down my legs, and a sense of peace and wholeness and cleansing and health . . . like when I was a child . . . it radiated through me. Jesus had healed me. I must go somewhere, I thought. Anywhere, away from the crowd. I need to feel it fully, to wallow in what had happened. I turned.

And then I heard the voice: "Who touched me?"

I froze, half standing, turned away from the voice.

"Who touched me?"

The crowd laughed. "In a crowd like this?!"

"Lord, twenty people are touching you at any time!"

"What are you talking about?!"

The voice again: "Someone touched me. I felt the power go out of me."

Everything in me wanted to run away, wanted to hide away so I wouldn't be exposed. They would cringe, jeer . . . the warmth would go. . . .

I turned, very slowly, shaking. My heart was beating in my ears, and I felt my head would burst. I knelt in front of Jesus. Eyes fixed on the dusty hem of his tunic, I forced myself to speak.

"I . . . I touched you. For years . . . twelve years, I have suffered. No one has been able to make me well. I was afraid. I thought if I asked you to heal me, your followers or maybe even you, would laugh at me or sneer. And I was afraid that if I touched you I would make you unclean. So I bent over and touched your hem. And now . . . I'm well."

I stared at the dusty material at the bottom of his robe. And then I felt Jesus' hands on my shoulders as he gently pulled me to my feet. He looked into my eyes, and the crowd seemed to disappear. I saw as he looked at me that he knew me, he knew the woman I was and wanted to be, he knew me so clearly—I shook my head. How, I asked myself—how did I think I could hide from you?

The warmth of his love was like the warmth of the sun. Wonder of wonders, he knew me and he loved me. "My daughter," he said, almost with a chuckle. "How could you make me unclean? You were right to reach out and touch me. Be whole . . . be strong . . . be free. . . ."

❧

The women sit, hushed. Martha finally breaks the silence.

"And then, you followed him."

"What else could I do? It wasn't as if I had much to leave. Following Jesus became my life."

Yes. The women sit and draw strength from Lydia's story. Jesus' touch was an intensely personal act of healing.

But the heart of Lydia's story is one that many preachers have missed. As Jesus touched Lydia, he performed an act of ritual cleansing, washing from womanhood the fear and degradation with which most religions have fouled it for centuries.[7]

And it was a summons to follow.

John said to me yesterday that I was courageous to come to Jerusalem with Jesus, to make the long journey, to stand at Golgotha and be known as one of his friends. I didn't understand him. What else could I do?

To Lydia it seems simple, natural to follow the teacher. But some of the women in the circle begin to look restless as they think of others who started the journey and turned aside. Martha speaks, trying as women often do, to soothe everyone, make them happy:

Lydia, you have been courageous. It upsets me . . . I wonder how his friends could desert him. But maybe we should have seen that our life with Jesus was completely new . . . that it was different for us. . . .

❧

Joanna has spoken only once before. She is the best educated of the women, the most finely dressed. Listed as one of the women who followed Jesus, Luke tells us that she was the wife of Herod's steward.[8] She finds her voice.

He said it would happen. Remember when he talked about the seeds . . .[9]

We were by the sea of Galilee and there were so many people that Jesus had to borrow someone's fishing boat. He sat in it waiting for the crowd to settle—mothers shushing babies, fathers quieting children, people sitting down—and Jesus pointed toward a farmer, who was walking through his field, reaching into his bag, pulling out seed and fanning it to the ground. We all watched him scoop and scatter on the hillside and Jesus started to talk about God's kingdom. As we listened he talked about the different kinds of ground on which the seed might fall. I could see the people in the crowd nodding their heads. Some seed, he said, fell on the path and birds ate it; some fell on rocky ground and it sprang up but then died; some fell among thorns which choked it; some fell into good soil and produced a wonderful crop. And it became clear as Jesus talked that he was using the seeds as symbols for God's word which was being scattered in all of us listeners.

Perhaps we were afraid to understand, for fear it would come to this.

But that day and the next, we saw his words fulfilled. We saw people who heard Jesus and shook their heads and went away. And others who got really excited, "What a great teacher we've got here! Will you listen to this guy!" but drifted as soon as Jesus challenged them to care for the poor or love their in-laws. And there were those who joined us, full of enthusiasm and zeal for a week or two and then with some great excuse—their families or their property or their health—they chose not to follow.

A new voice pulls the women back from the summer hillside and the voice of the teacher.

And there were some, like us, for whom the words of Jesus were life itself. We stretched our roots eagerly into his love.

Two

She holds a spindle in her lap, though it is still several hours before the Sabbath ends and she can use it. Her face wrinkles around the bright eyes in her small, almost childlike face. She is one who has been silenced by the forgetfulness of preachers and theologians.

Forgotten in life, forgotten for years by Christendom: she sits in this circle.[10] Rhoda. She looks around their faces and begins to speak:

For eighteen years I had been bent over, only able to see the ground in front of me.

How did it start? I have never been able to remember. . . . There were years of work—spinning (seems like I was born spinning), collecting firewood, pounding meal, cooking, making beds, washing clothes, looking after my sister's little children—it did seem as if I were always looking down.

And one day when I got up off my mat . . . who knows what had happened during the night? My body was twisted, like my life.

What could I do but carry on—finding firewood, pounding meal, looking after the children? It was not so bad as long as the children were small. But as they got bigger they jeered at me over my head, laughing, calling me names. Day in and day out, I heard the hoots and shrieks from the village children.

The worst part, my sisters, was that I could never see the sky. People talked about the moon and for years I could only catch a glimpse of it near the horizon, or I would hear the long swish of a bird flying overhead and wrench my neck, but it was gone.

And no faces. Eighteen years and no eyes smiling at me, no face searching mine to see how I felt. People addressed me as if I were deaf, or not even human, almost like a dog. After a year or two I hardly spoke; people couldn't hear me or didn't know I could speak; they didn't listen. I became silent.

And no touch. Villagers often embraced when they met, but how could they embrace me—twisted as I was?

My life became one of dust and dirt. And my stick, poking into the ground, became something like my friend. Sometimes I wondered as I was scratching along searching for firewood: What if I someday found something valuable —a coin perhaps—that someone had dropped so that I could buy a lovely piece of fabric to wear over my head? But day after day, the work, the dust, the stick. The possibility of a miracle disappeared.

I never talked to anyone, looked at anyone, touched anyone. I began to wonder if I were really human.

But my life was not all bad, my sisters. I had the Sabbath. That day I went with the rest of the villagers to the synagogue. I heard them greet one another. Occasionally somebody even mentioned me—that was a special day —"Well it looks like the Romans can't affect everything— the sun still rises and old Rhoda still hobbles along." They knew I was alive. Outside the synagogue I waited until everyone else had crowded in. Then I held my stick and moved to the back of the women's side. Ah, it was wonderful to hear the prayers and the scriptures, to hear about

Abraham and Sarah. It seemed to me that the earth floor of
the synagogue was different from the ground outside because of all the prayers that had soaked into it. And when I
said, "Amen" with the others in the synagogue—for a moment I was part of the community.

Then I heard that a new rabbi was going to be in the
synagogue that Sabbath. I'd overheard people talking about
him—some saying he was a wonderful healer, others that
he taught like no one else, some that he was dangerous
because he broke Sabbath rules, others that he was mad or
maybe demon-possessed. I knew I wanted to hear this rabbi
teach.

That Sabbath I hobbled toward the synagogue—dusty
step after dusty step, sun beating on my back. Other villagers were crowding around me, so I stopped outside, listening to snippets of conversation. "My cousin in Capernaum
says that the rabbis there were angry with him. . . ."

"A woman I know in Cana told me the most amazing
story about a wedding. . . ."

I could tell from the sounds and the dust that there
were more people than usual going into the synagogue.

I caught my breath. What if it were full? I waited for
the sound of feet to die away, and I heard the service begin.
"Hear, O Israel, the Lord your God is one God and you
shall love the Lord your God with all your heart . . ."

I moved toward the entrance but someone strode by,
pushing me aside. I heard someone else coming. More

footsteps rushed past. I listened. Outside it was quiet except for a few bees buzzing. Inside I could hear a voice begin to speak, one I'd never heard before. I couldn't understand the words. I needed to hear him. I started toward the door.

What if there is no space? I stopped. But the voice pulled me. How will I know where to move to find a place? I stumbled through the entrance.

I always moved toward the back of the women's section. This morning, where I usually saw bare floor, I could see only bottoms of tunics.

"Please . . ." I said, but no one moved. The voice was still speaking, but the words were lost to me. "Please . . ." Shame began to overwhelm me. This great teacher, and I was standing in the aisle. Perhaps distracting people. I stumbled forward a few steps, but more tunics, more tunics. "Please . . ." No space. No one moved.

I must leave, I thought, I must go outside. I felt people's stares. My eyes burning with tears, I turned and started toward the door, my stick leading me. To never hear this teacher, his words, his teaching. How could I ever come back into the synagogue?

As I reached the door, I felt a hand on my shoulder. "Listen," whispered a woman's voice. "He's calling you." My heart stopped. I listened and heard the murmur of the villagers:

"What in the world is the rabbi up to?"

"What does he want from her, it's just old Rhoda. . . ."

But above all these, I heard another voice: "Woman, come here."

The teacher couldn't be calling me. He must mean someone else. A great teacher would never call a woman, but if he did, it wouldn't be someone like me. One of the children cried out, "The rabbi's calling Old bent-back. Ha, ha."

And then another woman's voice: "Rhoda, he's calling you. Go and see what he wants." How long had it been since anyone had spoken to me?

My heart beating in my ears, my face still burning, I turned and started toward the front of the synagogue.

I felt all the eyes of the village burning into me, but the voice drew me on. "That's right. I won't hurt you. Come up here."

I reached the front of the synagogue. I could see the bottoms of the fine robes of the rulers of the synagogue as they sat in their places of honor. But I also saw a shabby tunic and dusty feet. I froze, staring at those feet.

His voice changed and became almost stern: "Woman, you are set free from your ailment."

And then I felt his hands, large and warm on my back. How long since someone had touched me? They felt solid, human . . .

I felt a warmth spreading from those hands throughout my body. I knew I must see his face. I dropped my stick and slowly pulled myself up, looking at his robe and then directly into his face. His eyes searched mine. The first hands to touch me, the first eyes to look into mine with love—they were the eyes of Jesus.

"Thank you," I said, still staring into his face. And then my joy overflowed.

"God be praised," I said. I don't know how I did it, but I turned to face the congregation . . . and of course they were a group of strangers—I hadn't seen them for so long.

"God be praised," I said to them. "Look at me. I'm straight. I stand before God because of this man." I turned to Jesus and he smiled. "Yes, God be praised," he said.

I turned to the rulers of the synagogue, trying to recognize the faces I'd last seen years before, eager to share my joy with them. But their faces—confused, shocked, angry.

"God be praised!" I said to them.

They looked at each other, and then the ruler of the synagogue stood. "Silence, woman," he said to me. "Women do not speak in the synagogue. You should know that."

He quieted the congregation, his voice cold. "There are six days on which work ought to be done; come on those days and be cured, and not on the Sabbath."

My mind reeled in the silence. The new rabbi could not have done wrong. I was whole. My face burned.

Jesus took a deep breath. "You hypocrites!" he said, his anger blazing. "Does not each of you on the Sabbath untie his ox or his donkey from the manger, and lead it away to give it water?" He turned to me and put his hand on my shoulder. "And ought not this woman, a daughter of Abraham whom Satan bound for eighteen long years, be set free from this bondage on the Sabbath day?"

That moment seemed to stretch. A daughter of Abraham . . . a child of promise. A daughter of Abraham. . . .

The ruler of the synagogue narrowed his eyes with hatred. But the villagers had taken up my cry "Praise God!" "God has visited his people." Straight and tall, I joined their praises. . . .

Rhoda sits silently for a few minutes. Like the others, she is trying to make sense of her story, now that the teacher is dead. She speaks again.

Jesus had called me a daughter of Abraham, and I loved the sound of that.[11] As I walked out of the synagogue I said it over and over to myself. Daughter of Abraham. Daughter of Abraham. Just outside, I heard two of the rulers of the synagogue. "Did you hear what he called her . . . a daughter of Abraham? Never has anyone said that. It is an insult to Abraham."

"All women are daughters of Eve," the other ruler answered.

I tried not to hear them. All that seemed to matter was that I was a daughter of Abraham. Jesus had said so.

But as I began to follow Jesus, I realized that for me to be a daughter of Abraham meant that Jesus brought new life not only for me. His message was also for others who had been shut outside. Why didn't I see that there would be many, just like that ruler of the synagogue, who wouldn't accept Jesus' new way easily?

❧

Moved by Rhoda's story, the women sit quietly, each lost in her own thoughts. It is Jesus' mother who breaks the silence with her quiet sobs.

Mary, whose son lies dead. The women gathered in this circle stand in awe of her pain.

Mary. It is difficult to meet her eyes without seeing how she is haunted. Haunted by the baby. Haunted by the child. Haunted by the man.

The groping tiny hands, his downy hair, the smell of her own milk as she nursed him.

Miriam strokes the older woman's arm, and Mary shakes her head.

I weep because your words are a balm to my heart. My sisters, I would speak to you.

From my earliest memories, I knew God as love. When the service in the synagogue began with the call to love God with our whole hearts, everything within me stirred and said yes. Day by day: God was with me, God was love, God was goodness.

When did I know? I knew he was special before his life began stirring within me.

When did I know it would come to this? Alas, I have suspected it since he was tiny.

When did I know that I would have to let go? That has been unending, exhausting torment.

I should have been ready, from the first visitation . . .[12]

I was young, my sisters, only fifteen. I was engaged to Joseph but that day I was in my parents' house, kneading bread when I heard, or perhaps felt, someone, something behind me. When I spun around, there was a presence. And it seemed to speak to me, telling me that I was blessed and would be visited by God.

Although I know God's presence and have known his love, my sisters, I was shocked and frightened. Why this special visitation? The presence calmed me, and seemed to speak of a son whom I should call Jesus, who would be a great teacher in Israel. I asked how this could happen, since I was unmarried. And then it seemed that I could see the presence more clearly. And a voice: "The Holy Spirit will come upon you, and the power of the Most High will overshadow you; therefore the child to be born will be holy; he will be called the Son of God."

Those words. They pulled me outside time. Before me loomed a most terrible choice. I could shake my head. The angelic presence would disappear, and my life would go on. I would finish kneading the bread and go to meet Joseph in the afternoon sunshine of the village square. No one else need ever know. . . . I would have children and we would live a contented life together in Nazareth. Occasionally as the months turned to years, I would remember the visitation and wonder what might have happened. After some years, I would begin to believe that I had dreamed it.

Or . . . or . . . I could say yes. And somehow the immense privilege and anguish of that yes seemed clear to me for a split second. I knew the pain would be appalling.

But I also knew God as love.

"Here I am," I said. "God's servant. I'm willing to be the bearer of this child."

Mary pauses drawing strength from that memory. How many times over the years has she stopped to remember this call?

I knew he was special.

Any birth is an overwhelming experience, pain too intense even for crying out; the crushing joy at the baby—squalling and messy but alive. Many of you know, my sisters, how after birth, it feels as if only two are left in the world. As I looked at his little head, hair plastered to it, and into his deep eyes, the world disappeared and only Jesus and I lived. I didn't wonder who he was, nor what he would come to. He cried lustily and suckled as if he were starved. I loved him, much like any other mother loves a firstborn child.

Who knows how much time passed? Joseph ushered in visitors, peasants who had been told of his birth. . . .[13] They crowded all around us, fear and excitement in their faces.

"Well look at him—first time I ever saw a king!"

"Sure the littlest one around, I'll wager."

"We saw a crowd of heavenly beings, having such a celebration, nearly scared my sandals off me, it did . . . so bright and beautiful."

Then came the time for the purification rites.[14] I remember laughing as I packed for the trip to the temple. According to the law of Moses I needed to be purified after childbirth, before I could touch anything holy. And for all these days I had been holding and suckling the holiest one of all.

He was such a lovely baby, and I felt proud to be a mother bearing her infant son toward the temple.

I carried Jesus in the southern gate of the temple when an ancient man rushed through the eastern gate, searching. Then he smiled and moved straight toward us. He reached out and took Jesus from me and prayed, telling God he was ready to die, because his old eyes had seen the savior. He slowly handed Jesus back to me and blessed us solemnly. Then he looked at me and shook his head painfully. He spoke words that I've never forgotten: "This child is destined for the falling and the rising of many in Israel. . . . And a sword will pierce your own soul, too."[15]

❧

Many times I have thought that Simeon's words were being fulfilled—times that my heart ached with the pain of this special child. But yesterday as they crucified him . . .

Mary closes her eyes. The little bundle of flesh in her arms and the mangled flesh on the cross mingle for a moment. She takes a deep breath and speaks.

There were many reminders that this, my firstborn, was a holy child. Even as old Simeon turned away, a very old woman named Anna, known for her holiness, came to me. She also knew who Jesus was, and began to praise God.[16]

Others, not of our faith, worshipped him.[17] So you see I was reminded over and over again that he was special and he was not mine. Sometimes I found myself holding him and wishing, desperately, that he was an ordinary baby, one I could love as my own.

I saved up my questionings and my wonderings. Sometimes I lay in the dark and mulled over them.

As a boy he grew up like other children. Sometimes I almost forgot who he was, when he came in muddy from playing in the stream.

Jesus was like a dream child. As mothers we dream our children's lives, as they suckle at our breasts. We see their trust, their innocence, their delight with a spring flower, a sunset. And we think maybe this child will not have to wander, will not be lost.

But all children are lost to us, except perhaps those who die in infancy. The child begins to choose death: the mother hears her tell a first lie. She hears her speak to hurt or tease. Or she sees his rapt horror as he watches someone hurt a fly or a mouse. His fascination with swords. She looks into the child's eyes and realizes they are clouded by death, from that first death of our parents in the garden.

The mother understands that the child of her dreams, the one who was able to love without dilution, has vanished and can never be found again. And she wonders: "What might he have been, had he not disappeared forever?" "How might she have lived if she had not been twisted by life?"

Jesus never did that. That desolation of the child slipping deeper and deeper into self-absorption and away from love—it never happened. That was a wonder. But it was frightening, because I knew that the world hates what is truly good.[18]

Yesterday, I thought of the days and nights when Jesus was small and we had to flee south. I with my fear of Herod, trying to keep Jesus from crying out.[19] And those other mothers whose babies were killed . . . I wondered if maybe it was easier for them—they lost their sons over thirty years ago. I had to learn to lose my son; they never had to give them up except to the sword. I thought of him as my own; I was the only one who really understood the wonder of who he was—this terrible secret that only Jesus and I shared.

The women sit in silence. Having heard his mother speak, what can they say?

THREE

Mary Magdalene sits quietly, but her serenity is only skin deep. Sometimes she breathes quickly as panic overtakes her. A tear runs down her cheek, a shiver passes through her body, and it seems that she is only a heartbeat away from flight. At any moment she might struggle to her feet and run—rushing toward oblivion. But instead she sits like marble, occasionally reaching her hand out to clasp that of the old woman who sits next to her.

Mary looks into her lap, as if she is listening to two voices: the soft speaking of the women around her, and the shriek of terror that echoes within. Her blood warms as she hears the women speak and then freezes as she is pulled back to the tomb: his deafening silence, his caking blood.

Mary Magdalene. For centuries she has fascinated people as a loose woman and a prostitute, even though Luke only tells us that seven demons came out of her and she followed Jesus.[20]

Mary Magdalene was not a prostitute, but a young woman straining at the confines of her culture's restrictions on women, and God alone knows how many women like her have been driven to madness over the centuries. Her reputation as a prostitute has been propagated by men who wanted to believe that anything might be possible of a woman who won a place so near the Christ.[21]

No, Mary Magdalene had the misfortune to be born brilliant, sensitive, and profound in a time when only boys could be educated, when to teach a girl the Torah was unacceptable.[22] As she grew up she noticed nuances that washed over others. Sitting in any gathering, the complex interplay of loves and hates and fears seemed to bawl at her. And seeing so much, she felt alien, as if she were outside looking in. The other women in her home—aunts, sisters, and servants—seemed to enjoy simple pleasures and she felt as if she were being dragged deeper in an undertow of overwhelming passions and bitter certainties.

Mary Magdalene survived impossible years of not finding the words to express her doubts and terrors, of wondering if she were mad, of shame when she didn't fit.

She was vulnerable. And then there must have been an incident that opened her up to a desperate, suicidal act, when she began to throw herself away. Perhaps it was sexual, but the sexual sin was simply a door to the greater sin of treating herself like garbage. She believed a lie about herself—that her value was only skin deep, to be found in her beauty and sexuality. She lost herself and started to slip away.

Mary Magdalene pulls herself up straight. She has just enough strength to drag herself out of the cacophony of her inner world and speak. She looks around the circle, and begins:

I owe . . . all I am and all I have to him. I cannot believe he is dead. But . . .

This is hard for me to say to you, my sisters . . . the pain and horror at Golgotha yesterday . . . it was not as black and awful as the months or years of my life before I met him. This morning as I was waking . . . and a few times yesterday in my deepest despair, I felt a touch of the old terror. But even in the darkness, we know that light exists.

Mary Magdalene has broken silence. Naming the light, she finds she can tell her story.

When I think back to my life before I met him—it is like a glimpse of another world. There were no idyllic childhood days. My mother died when I was only very young, and no matter where I was, who I was with—I could see darkness lurking just under the surface. My blood sisters never seemed to struggle. One by one I saw them marry, my father proudly giving his blessing. But I was always haunted by premonitions of the harsh realities which would soon slip over those superficial happy faces. The beginnings of a twisting envy in my widowed aunt, the agony my sister would know in childbirth, the devastation of her husband when she died. These cruel certainties washed over the cheerful facade of any scene I witnessed.

My father bemoaned what he called my boy's brain—more than a girl deserved or needed. When I met a suitor, I knew it should be enough that he wanted a connection with our family, that he would make me a mother of children, that he looked at my body with longing. But the truth that I was never valued tore at me.

One evening brought a turning point, although I could not have seen it at the time. I had been sitting with my sister; her first baby was expected soon. It was twilight when I started home, and I took a shortcut near the market. I expected it to be empty, but some people were there whom I had only ever seen from a distance—the crowd that enjoys the largesse of the tax collectors. They were laughing together, and they shouted to me. I should join them for a drink of wine, to celebrate, they said. I knew I should keep walking, but I stopped. "What are you celebrating?" I asked, without turning. "The full moon," they shouted. "Stop and look at it." The laughter, and the whimsy of celebrating beauty drew me; I thought of going home where father likely had some fat old suitor wheezing as he waited for me. I told myself that I deserved a little pleasure, just for a few minutes. And that first evening, it was only that.

When I got home, father was furious. Such an important man had waited to see me, and then had left in disgust —how would he look? I knew I could never tell him. But how he didn't hear in little Magdala,[23] of my double life— that, I thought, was a miracle. I met with my friends, as I came to think of them, especially Stephen—he was the bastard son of a Jewish woman and a Greek teacher. At home I lived the life of a respectable Jewish virgin. My father encouraged me to meet suitors, old widowers who wanted a respectable connection. I looked at them mockingly as I thought of Stephen's bulging shoulders, his eagerness to kiss and fondle me.

And then the nightmares started. It was almost as if my selves were tangling. I dreamed I was with an old suitor at our house, and I began to stroke him and bare my breasts. His face would fill with shock and horror and he would call my father, shouting, "A whore, she's a whore. . . ." Or I dreamed that I was with my marketplace friends and that Stephen would tell them all that he could no longer find anything to give me; I had ruined his fertility because I was a witch. The dreams continued until I could not disentangle them from reality.

One tormented morning I woke from nightmare-ridden sleep and wandered away from Magdala, along the coast of the sea of Galilee . . . and then my memory fades and I remember nothing but the horror . . . the torment. . . .

❧

Mary Magdalene pauses. The gathered women will not ask her to plumb the depths of her darkness; they've heard whispers about it. But she feels, perhaps more than any other, the wonder in this room on this Sabbath. All that they tell each other—the horrors and the healings—are part of the story. Mary Magdalene wants them to know. She looks around the room as the late afternoon sun plays on their faces.

The terror and the darkness . . .

You must know, that in spite of his death, the world is light now compared with the darkness of evil.

How can I even begin to describe it?

As the women watch Mary Magdalene, she closes her eyes and shakes her head. Beads of sweat appear on her upper lip as she remembers what she has desperately tried to forget.

The tormented one . . . was it me?

Her eyes are distant as she tells what she has never told before.

❧

Dark, dark, dark. Horror, trembling fear coldly clutching her stomach, retching always retching as if food were too wholesome to stay in her hell. Tearing at her hair, cutting at her filthy skin, her hated tissue, wrenching off her cursed private parts, nausea and retching. Swirling, vomiting blackness. Hate her. Hate her, afraid of her: run from her, chasing wildly away from her, but never away. Chained, stitched to her in the blackness of night and the blackness of day. Chained and stitched by frozen black chains. Wrenching away and falling, falling, falling. Twisting and wrenching away from her. Her smell of rotting corpses in a hot marketplace. When she claws her flesh, her blood smells of death and flies and maggots crawling, searching over her eyes and nose; rats pushing in and out of her vagina. With every twist, every retch, every rip at flesh, she knew this darkness was always, always. Forever vomiting, rotting corpses, darkness twisting, howling through eternity . . .

And then the voice.

Too late. She's gone, gone, gone . . . a black speck on the horizon . . . no one can ever find her and pull her back. Chained to the rotting corpses . . . in the darkness pulled down, down, down . . . nothingness and death . . .

The voice. Mary. A glimmer of light, the scent of a wild rose, the touch of a warm hand. Mary.

The wild shrieking voices, wailing louder, screaming. "Let us alone . . . don't kill us. . . ." Fury of battle, pulling, dashing, flinging, wrenching her apart.

"Be silent and come out of her." Slicing, amputation, limb from limb, organs jerked out, screaming and wailing.

And then silence. Floating on nothingness. Warmth, trembling, wounds closing, knitting together. Sunshine melting.

Minutes or hours later, I opened my eyes. There was love. Deep brown eyes stared into mine. I was known. I was loved. Mary. Known and loved. Known and loved. Named. Mary.

She looks around at her sisters, her terrors quelled as she relives her awakening.

Did he say anything? He brushed my hair out of my mouth and touched my forehead. Did he say "Follow me"? I heard him say it to others later.

Perhaps he knew that he didn't have to say it to me; I knew that I'd follow him anywhere, even to death.

He smoothed my hair and then moved to speak to a woman nearby. It was you, Susannah. You came over to where I was sprawled on the ground. You put your arm around my shoulders and looked at me with . . . I know

now it was compassion. I can't remember what you said to me. . . .

The old woman next to Mary Magdalene holds her hand like a lifeline. This is Susannah, mentioned by Luke as one of Jesus' women disciples. As Mary Magdalene has told her story, Susannah has listened, riveted like a mother watching her child on a stage, mouthing each word, nodding with each movement.

As she has finished her story, old Susannah's face crinkles; her eyes brim over. She loves Mary. She has kept silent until now, but she longs to join in the story, to tell her part as it intertwines with Mary's. And so together they tell of the first days of Mary's new life, talking back and forth to each other, almost as lovers do.

"I told you to come along and we'd get you washed up and into some fresh clothes ready to start your new life. I said I'd give you something to eat. And you burst into tears."

"Yes. I was so afraid . . . that I'd never see him again . . . that love would escape me . . . And you told me . . . that his name was Jesus . . . and you said he'd never leave us. . . ."

The words pull at the women. Never leave us. . . .

Susannah breaks into the quiet. Although she speaks to Martha and Maria, she looks at Mary Magdalene.

Martha, you and Maria cannot imagine our lovely Mary as she was then. She was like a newborn—messy, but altogether innocent. I tried to talk to you, dearie, while we got the bath ready, asking what you'd heard about him . . . but of course you hadn't been in a fit state to hear anything. I told you he was from Nazareth, and that his mother shared your name, and that he'd worked as a carpenter for a number of years . . . you stared at me as if I were speaking Greek.

You said we'd have to burn my clothes. And when I was in the bath you started to talk about John the Baptist[24] and that really scared me.

I was chattering away to distract you from the state you were in. Just when I was trying to figure out what to do with your hair, I thought of John's sheepskin and tried to describe him to you. I told you that he was a bit of a wild man—seemed to me that might make you feel better —how he roared at people that they were unworthy, unready for the Messiah, about how they needed to stop being so greedy and heartless to each other and repent of their wickedness.

I told you about John's baptism and the idea of making a clean start, just like we were helping you do . . . and that some had thought John was the Messiah—while I was chopping out great chunks of your hair, which clearly hadn't been touched in months—and asked him, and John said he wasn't worthy to untie the sandals of the Messiah.

The sun has moved down the western sky and shines on the old woman's face as Mary Magdalene listens to her and then speaks.

And this phrase stuck in my mind—that the Messiah would baptize, not with water, but with the holy spirit and fire. This brutal Messiah that you were talking about: all power, holiness, judgment. I shivered as you lopped away. . . .

You've got to admit that your hair needed it and it looked nice afterward. And then we found you some clean clothes. And I told you that the Messiah was Jesus.

You told me not to look so frightened. That name had only become more and more dear to you from the first day you'd heard it, and it was already beloved to me, even though I'd met him less than two hours before. I was terrified of the Messiah. I thought he'd be like God—an old man, awful in his judgment, demanding more and more. That the Christ would hate and destroy me.

Then you made me stand up and you said, "Clean and fresh as a newborn, and ready to start the new life. . . ." And that's how I felt.

I fell into a deeper sleep than I ever remember having. Hours later when I started to drift awake, I was terrified. It felt as if the shalom, the freedom, the light in my soul were an impossible, wonderful dream which had gotten lost and drifted somehow into my nightmare world. I started to shriek.

I told you that Jesus and some of his followers had gone off to help some other people and that they'd be back soon, and that our job in the meanwhile was to get you healthy and well—lots of food and rest.

I watched you kneading your dough, Susannah. You said you thought Jesus might be back the next day, and we could make bread for him and for the others who were traveling with him.

You taught me to grind the wheat, which I'd always thought of as servants' work. And you began telling me some of his stories. I especially remember one about a woman making bread; Jesus said that God's presence was like the yeast she put into the dough which spread until the loaf was raised. You told me other stories Jesus told about God's new way—that it was like a woman searching and searching for a coin, finding it, and calling her friends to a party. That it was like discovering treasure or a priceless pearl and giving away everything to have it.[25]

Mary Magdalene smiles. Her first smile in this circle. Is it the wonder of this teacher telling such stories, even stories that embrace the lives of women as no other rabbi had ever done? Or is it simply the light of those early memories of traveling with the teacher? She sits up straighter as she goes on.

Those first weeks following Jesus are like my earliest memories, blurred, with a vivid recollection here and there, and so much I didn't understand. I wanted to be near him, so I went wherever Jesus was teaching and helping people. He loved the sweaty, smelly crowds that swarmed around him, some with matted hair and weeping sores; some dressed in rags. I watched him all the time, as he looked from one to the next, like each was a long-lost friend; he touched them with his big carpenter hands.

And his words. He told us that the world was exactly the opposite of what we'd thought. That it is the poor, the hungry, the ones who've struggled who are really fortunate because God is on their side. That as his friends it doesn't matter if the powerful shut us out, because in that way we are like the holy prophets of old. The people in power have had their day in the sun, he said. And he taught us about a new way of life—as we learned to love people, even those who had hurt or abused us, how we were to learn to forgive and to give.[26]

It was so new, and I was so new. . . . He said we could talk to God like a parent, and the teachers in the crowd winced. I could almost hear my father muttering, "What will people get up to if they think God loves them?" Jesus said that we should tell God our concerns and that it was our spiritual treasure that would last, not our houses or clothes. He told us not to worry. God will care for us just as he paints the flowers lovely with colors and feeds the birds that fly and nest. God will look after us.

Mary Magdalene's smile fades as she remembers.[27] *New spiritual experiences, and everything seems so clear. But seekers down the ages know that the life of faith is not simple. The convert is not made new in one brush stroke. As she lives the new life, she discovers that she has brought herself, her painful upbringing, the stories she's been told, along with her. She makes distressing discoveries and must seek healing over and over again.*

Sometimes I almost forgot what I had been—it seemed like another life or another world. But then some specter would jump out and frighten me. Perhaps six months after I'd become a disciple, a group of us were walking toward Capernaum, and we met a possessed man being held by four men. He was like a wild animal, thrashing around, squalling and barking. A crowd gathered.

And my heart seemed to stop. Half a year before I was that crowd-entertaining wild creature. For months, years, I didn't even know how long . . . they had laughed and gawked at me.

"Wow, will you look at that. I wish my Levi could see this; won't he be jealous when we tell him?"

"One of the best I've seen and I've seen a good many in my time . . . strong . . . look at him—those four can barely hold him."

"Sounds likes a wild donkey being branded . . . hard to beat this for entertainment."

I turned away, covering my face

Possession: ultimate loss of control, terminal abuse. Mary Magdalene is haunted by lost years of a life. She can never be sure who gawked at her nakedness; she has no idea what she has done, what was done to her. Even now, she shudders, and swallows hard before she speaks.

Then the man tore himself away from the ones who were holding him and dashed toward us. He froze, screeching, and Jesus spoke like thunder. "Come out of him immediately." And the man dropped like a rag doll. Jesus moved to him. He knelt and stroked his cheek, waiting for him to come around. By now I was crying.

The man opened his eyes. He rolled onto his back and looked at us. He smiled. "Good morning. Or is it afternoon? Whichever it is, I'm hungry."

It was his first moment in the world, like watching the birth of a baby.

Mary Magdalene smiles at a memory which is sacramental for her: his deliverance renews hers.

Then she shakes her head. How could one who did these miracles . . . ?

The women stir as they remember this scene. For some it is not a sacrament, but a fearsome portent, the day when they began to sense the struggle. The crowd had celebrated and the religious leaders had became colder and more threatened. Susannah, so close to Mary Magdalene, would remember only a sense of victory.

The crowd went wild, shouting "The Son of David!" "Who else could do such miracles?" "The Messiah has visited us!"

Joanna frowns. She had seen in this moment the seeds of the teacher's death. Jesus' deliverance of a demonized person was considered to be the most dramatic demonstration that God's power was with him,[28] and Jesus' simple rescue frightened the religious leaders. Joanna speaks.

I remember. One of the teachers—a ruler of the local synagogue—stepped forward. He hushed the crowd and said, yes, it was amazing, but people needed to remember that there were two kinds of power: God's power and the power of evil. As teachers, he implied, they could help people figure out which was good and which was bad power. Then another teacher pointed to the group of followers standing near Jesus. "Look what kind of people this "Messiah" of yours associates with. Then ask where he gets his power."

The crowd was murmuring when Jesus held his hand up. He spoke quietly, but with tremendous authority. He told the teachers that you can't cast Satan out in the name of Satan. Then he paused and stared at them, and I could see their faces turn white as he continued: "But if I by the spirit of God cast out demons, then the Kingdom of God has come to you."

He was pushing their backs to the wall, forcing them to choose.

What they witnessed that day was a struggle for power. Not only a spiritual battle with demonic forces, but also a battle between earthly powers of good and evil. Jesus' power suggested that God was on his side, and Jesus associated with bad types: common people, not very respectable; many women; few from the normal echelons of power or the best families. If these were God's chosen, then the religious authorities were in trouble.

If Jesus were the Messiah . . . it couldn't be. The kingdom of God had to be on the religious establishment's own terms. The women are silent, grasping, some for the first time, what Jesus' ministry, liberating for the poor and the oppressed, meant for him. Joanna speaks again.

Jesus taught us that if our eyes were clear, our whole vision would be full of light. Our vision was clouded before we met Jesus, through our own fault and the fault of others. Our sight was healed by his power and compassion. But at the same time his acts of mercy kept us from seeing, as clearly or as soon as we might have—where Jesus' new way would lead him.

It's hard to imagine how and when any of Jesus' followers would have begun to see that he would be killed, that he was on a collision course with the religious authorities. But for the women . . . everything was so new.

Like many women, they had been valued as wives of husbands and bearers of children, as beautiful bodies. But beyond that, they had been taught that to be a woman was to be a daughter of Eve, a temptress. They had learned, almost from the womb, that they were a threat to men, that men could only be safe from their sexual pollution by avoiding them.[29]

What would it take to counteract all those Sabbaths, sitting in another part of the synagogue so that you didn't distract or pollute men? What would it take to wipe out the years of temple apartheid—using a separate entrance and keeping a distance from the holy places, because men could approach God as you, a woman, never could?

Jesus encouraged the women to follow him, teaching them, asking them serious theological questions, demanding a response from the mind and heart—all of this, and yet it must have been hard to relearn. Mary Magdalene must have felt over-whelmed. . . .

The world seemed so new. Simple. But I hadn't reckoned on all that I carried with me into the new life. When Joanna came to join us, after I'd been following several months, I began to see.

Joanna, you were beautiful and wore lovely clothes; I knew that your husband was a steward for Herod.[30]

Mary Magdalene must have been the stunning new convert for months. People would have whispered when they entered a village. "That one—she's the one . . . they say there were seven demons. . . ." Joanna must have replaced Mary Magda-lene as the star, and all the lessons of competing for men's atten-tion, which women learn from the cradle, surfaced.

Luke tells his readers that Mary Magdalene, Joanna, Susan-nah and many other women were with Jesus and supported the group out of their resources. To prepare food for the teacher was a labor of love, which the women did with a sense of joy and privi-lege. After all, not only had most rabbis never allowed women to follow them or even listen to their teaching, they had not allowed

*women to provide food for them. Women were so frequently un-
clean, and could lead men astray so readily: men would too easily
be contaminated by them.*

*Perhaps their jealousy surfaced when the women were baking
for Jesus and the followers at Susannah's home.*

When Joanna came to help us with the evening meal,
I found myself wishing she hadn't become a follower. I
pictured her sitting by Jesus, listening to him, taking my
place.

Joanna, it seems so long ago, I can barely remember
what my jealousy felt like. Deep inside me, a wraith stirred
and reminded me that I could attract a man because I was
beautiful; I could make him do my bidding because he
wanted me. I watched you and Susannah working and I
was filled with poison.

Susannah, you know my soul as well as you know
your own. The next day you sent Joanna off with the food
and then you sat me down and asked me to tell you what
was wrong.

I couldn't do it. You'd done so much for me, loving
me back to health, and I thought if you saw what was
lurking in me, you'd despise me. Finally I managed to tell
you about my lust, my fear, my jealousy, my hatred.

I waited for you to be shocked. Instead you reminded
me that we were becoming new people. My great fear—I
realized it then—was that I might not be able to change and
grow. You said we all had as much to unlearn as we had to
learn.

You helped me see for the first time that as his disciples, we were creating a new society, a new world, one in which men and women could work together and care for one another without using each other. I felt excited.

But I also felt vulnerable: I'd been stripped of my most powerful weapon, one that I'd always carried with me. I cried on your shoulder, Susannah. I asked you how we could possibly unlearn the lessons we'd been taught all our lives.

And you said, "That's why Jesus is here."

We cried together because it all seemed so wonderful and so frighteningly new and impossible, and then Joanna came in and found us crying and we told her what we'd been talking about.

We stayed up until dawn. Joanna, you told me how miserable you'd been with your fancy clothes, lovely house, your children and an overpowering emptiness. When I went to bed that night I wondered how things would turn out for us. You'd left everything, Joanna. I had to believe God would look after you, after us. Susannah, you were so good to Joanna and me—kind and wise.

Susannah looks at Mary Magdalene, her face radiant with a love that sometimes runs between women who have grown together. Susannah smiles all around the room.

My story isn't as dramatic as yours, dear, but I too was delivered. I had been a lonely, selfish, old fool, ever since I lost my sons. I was totally turned in on myself. Sometimes I still am crotchety, but I'm a new person. And helping Mary was like helping a wounded beast by feeding, cleaning, and loving her; it helped me in my new life too.

They sit in silence for a few minutes. Almost all daylight has faded as Mary Magdalene has told her story. She pulls her tunic around her and bows her head under the weight of another memory.[31]

A week or two later we were in Capernaum. Jesus had been invited to supper at Simon the Pharisee's house. A number of us stood near one of the window openings, hoping to hear him teach. Jesus sat while Simon and his friends discussed how God would judge tax collectors for their knowledge of the Torah. Susannah whispered to me, "Now they'll see who the real teacher is."

But just as Jesus opened his mouth to speak, there was a stirring and murmuring near the door and someone moved into the room. The discussion at the table stopped abruptly. I was shocked—we all were—to see a prostitute, coming into a Pharisee's house. I felt afraid for her and for some reason, afraid for Jesus. Afraid for myself. A servant girl giggled. Everyone looked at Jesus.

The woman moved to stand behind him. The teachers around the table stiffened and looked at each other; several folded their arms across their chests. One put his hands over his eyes as if to protect himself. She stared at Jesus for—I don't know how long—it must have been a minute or two.

Time seemed almost to stop. The woman knelt at Jesus' feet and she began to cry. She stroked them, wiping away the day's dust with her tears. Then still weeping, she reached up and pulled a clip out of her hair so that it fell below her waist. She drew her hair over his feet, drying them. Each tear, each tender movement of her hands brimmed with love. Then she reached into her tunic and pulled out a small alabaster jar. She opened it and a wonderful scent filled the room. She knelt again and rubbed the ointment on them. She paused for a moment, and then kissed each of his feet just above his toes. . . . I think she kissed them right where the nails went yesterday. . . . Then she bowed and moved a few feet away and knelt.

"A real prophet would know better than to let her touch him."

"Makes you wonder how many tricks she turned to pay for that perfume."

"Doesn't seem to matter to him how she got the money—how many laws she broke."

"And now he's unclean from her touching him. . . . Practically takes away one's appetite."

I was overcome with rage. These men knew nothing of what it is like to be ignored, spat at, treated like filth. They knew nothing of what it is like to be scorned and laughed at as if you do not exist. They knew nothing of what drove a woman to the streets.

Then the heat of my rage turned to ice. That woman was all women; we all knelt beside him. She was me. What would Jesus say to defend her, to defend me—my desperate mistakes, my wasted years, my turning from bad choices, my devotion—would he condemn? Would he say nothing?

Years seemed to pass before Jesus spoke. "Simon, I have something to say to you."

"Speak teacher," said Simon. And Jesus told him a

story about a creditor who had two men who owed him money—one five hundred denarii and the other fifty. And the creditor canceled their debts. Jesus asked Simon which would love the man more. And Simon answered that he thought probably the one who had the big debt canceled. And Jesus said, "Right."

Then he turned toward the woman whose head was still bowed over her knee. He spoke, looking at her as he rebuked Simon for offering him no water for his feet, no kiss, no oil for his head, while the woman had washed his feet with her tears, and kissed his feet and anointed them with ointment. "And so Simon," Jesus said, "her sins, which were many, have been forgiven, for she has shown great love. The one who has been forgiven little has shown little love."

He walked to the woman's side and touched her shoulders. She looked up, eyes streaming with tears. "Your sins are forgiven."

I don't think she even heard the murmur around the table, people muttering about the very idea of talking to a woman with her reputation, comparing her with a respectable man like Simon, and humans forgiving sin.

Jesus spoke over the grumbling. "Your faith has saved you. Go in peace."

The woman looked at Jesus with steady eyes. She smiled slightly and then moved from the room. I turned to Susannah, tears flowing down my face. "Let's go," I said. I didn't understand that his response to this woman would mean his death.[32]

FOUR

It is growing dark, and Martha stands and moves to the kitchen. Sabbaths have always been difficult for her, but this one has been the worst.[33] Now the Sabbath is over and she lights two small oil lamps and brings them into the room. They sit and watch the tiny flickers from the lamps and think about the darkness outside.

Once again the shadow of his death has spread itself over the room where the women are gathered. Neither his life nor his death can ever be theological dogma for these women. Jesus was not a wonderful revelation or a great teacher or even the Messiah. Jesus has turned their lives inside out. Joanna speaks again.

Jesus made it clear that the new wine wouldn't fit into old wineskins—that the old wineskins would burst if you put new wine in them.[34] He said that the new wine needed fresh skins.

Jesus' touch on Mary Magdalene's life, Rhoda's life, on Lydia's life, on my life—it brought healing and love. But our love for Jesus and his love for us cracked the whole mold of our existence wide open.

Joanna sees what many of these women mercifully don't. Within a month or two the male disciples can begin to put the pieces of their lives back together. Matthew can go into some respectable financial work. Peter and the others can go back to fishing. But these women, who have followed a religious teacher, traveled in mixed company, left their families to follow Jesus—for them there is no going back. With the death of the teacher, a door of freedom and meaning has slammed shut.

The woman alone is an anomaly, a fearful prophet, re-

minding each man of his impending death. For other women she is an insinuation of looming loneliness.

The women gathered here on this Holy Saturday had given their primary allegiance to Jesus and a radical new way of life as his disciples. How could they go back to being passive listeners, receiving their meaning secondhand or thirdhand? Their teacher is dead and their lives as they know it have also ended. They've left all, given all.

The women sit quietly, as the last tinges of the anointing fragrance move from the room. Susannah breaks the silence.

We had no choice but to follow him.

On this, the first day after his death, the other disciples have made their presence felt in this gathering of women. Yesterday they were the empty spaces; today they are the absences, the gaps. How can these women begin to come to terms with the waiting, watching, and agonizing which was not shared?

It is Salome who speaks her outrage about those who did not follow. She stands and puts her hands on her hips.

Who says we had no choice but to follow him? We could have listened and rambled off like so many others. We might have plotted to kill him. Or taken a nap when he asked us to sit with him. We might have run away when things looked dangerous. Or not showed up for his death. Think of the ones who weren't there yesterday. . . . Only

John managed to hang around. . . . We were all scared. I'll admit it.

Salome hits her hands together angrily. Rhoda speaks.

You must remember that we saw more clearly than they did. . . .

She pauses as if she is afraid to speak.

Where is Peter?

This outsider, who they thought was one of them. Where is he? Martha knows the details. Especially in a time of crisis, she is the one who would make it her business to find out.

Lazarus and John set out before the Sabbath sundown to try to find him. John came round to check on Jesus' mother, and said he was afraid Peter might take his life. They sent a message that they were all staying in Jerusalem with James.

Poor Peter. Having said he would stick with Jesus no matter what, he swore that he'd never heard of him, and then saw Jesus being taken away. . . .

Never able to make things right with him.

Susannah's statement stirs compassion in the women. Never able to make things right with him. Lydia shakes her head at the horror of this. Joanna speaks.

Peter was afraid to even try to understand what Jesus' teaching would mean. For almost as long as I've known him, he seemed to be trying to convince himself that Jesus couldn't be hurt.

I first saw his desperation when a number of them had come back across the sea of Galilee. Peter was tying up his boat and he called for Mary Magdalene and me to wait.

"What a few days!" he shouted to us from the beach. He walked up and told us the whole story. There was a big storm, he said. Huge waves and he knew the boat would sink and they would all be goners. "And where was Jesus in all this?" he rolled his eyes. "Sleeping like a baby in the front of the boat."

"He didn't even seem concerned that we were all going to die!" Then Peter told us how Jesus woke up and stopped the wind. His voice dropped almost to a whisper. This was very reassuring for Peter. Jesus could make a storm stop. Healing a leper, delivering Mary Magdalene—they seemed amazing—but to Peter anyone who could stop a storm . . .

He went on to tell us about a demonized man in the area of the Gerasenes,[35] and how they tried to chain him up and he broke the chains, and about his howls and bruises and the clanking and shrieks when he saw Jesus; and then how Jesus healed the man and sent the demons off into a herd of pigs that rushed down the hill into the sea—Peter really enjoyed painting the picture for us. The man was fine—Mary Magdalene had to ask Peter about that—said he sat there with a smile on his face and the townspeople who arrived hardly recognized him. And the pig-owner was furious, and all the people asked Jesus to leave.

Salome shakes her head again.

I can hardly believe it. Please go, please go—not just the pig-owner, but the people of the area. Sending the Messiah away, because he was disrupting their routines, their business. . . .

Joanna speaks.

I didn't want to think what that meant for Jesus. . . . But what impressed Peter was Jesus' show of power.

Sometimes Peter did seem to understand. Do you remember the day after Jesus prayed over the fish and bread and fed the crowd he'd been teaching? I wanted to take Jesus aside and tell him that people might misunderstand that kind of miracle and maybe he should limit himself to private ones. . . .

But feeding the people caught Peter's imagination. He was like a puppy bouncing around. After that when we were walking along, Jesus asked us what people said about him, and then asked us what we thought and before anyone could get a word out, Peter answered that Jesus was the Messiah, the son of the living God. Hearing him say it like that made all of us feel a little scared and proud of Peter for stating it so clearly. . . .

Less than an hour later, Jesus started to talk about suffering and dying. It was a warm summer afternoon, but there on the road the light suddenly dimmed. I hated what he said. I wanted to say, "Oh, teacher, must it be that way?" But Peter said to Jesus—in his bravest, gruffest voice: "That could never happen to you, Lord; I wouldn't let it."

And Jesus told him to get away, that he wasn't on God's side but the side of evil.

We were all shaken. Jesus went on to talk again about what it was like to be his follower, how we were to put him before our families and how we couldn't try to follow him and keep looking back. But it seemed to me that the warm day had turned frigid.

It didn't help that Peter and Judas talked so much. Judas was convinced that Jesus was exhausted from over-work, and that once he got rested up he'd get back his early enthusiasm and his upbeat preaching style and his vision for a new world, rather than all this obsessive teaching about suffering and death. Peter himself told me that he thought Jesus gave the wrong impression when he told people that they should deny themselves and take up their crosses to follow him. Peter thought they should join up first and experience Jesus' wonderful new kingdom, and then if he had to speak about suffering it would be part of the whole. Like he said, if you hear Jesus talking about losing your life and then see him walking on water then it all balanced out.

I don't think that Peter thought Jesus was going to die until he was arrested. We saw it, but the others didn't. That's why this last week has been so utterly shocking for them.

Salome stands next to the circle of women. Even in the soft lamplight, she looks like a strong, no-nonsense woman, one who is used to defending herself. She has spoken out angrily, but now she falters.

How can I tell you this, my sisters?

She covers her face with her hands and begins to cry.[36]

I am angry at the other disciples. Perhaps more angry than you because I myself am a slow learner. This is my confession: It was only yesterday, by the cross, that I started to understand.

Salome stops her sobs and looks around the women, her mouth set.

Jerusalem's religious leaders . . . I wonder how they are feeling today. Maybe they're rubbing their hands, thinking they have eliminated a simple rabbi with a dangerous message.

I began to see the deep truth of Jesus' message—what he was giving and what he was demanding—when he was on the cross.

You all seemed to understand so clearly. But until nearly the end, I was like Peter, I was like Judas. I wanted Jesus to stop moaning about suffering and giving things up and get on with setting up a kingdom.

That's why I encouraged James and John to join him. Their father, only a couple of months before he died, told me that Jesus had called James and John. I was upset. Until I heard him teach. Then I thought that this rabbi's message —it was so fresh and powerful—made him the kind of guy they should get close to.

How could I have been so blind? Especially after their father died, I felt that part of being a good mother was giving them the advice they needed and a push now and then. Especially because John was a sensitive boy . . .

It's hard for me to say this. I felt they were being overlooked, or maybe they didn't see that you had to push to get ahead, and so I pushed them . . . told them they should get a promise from Jesus about places in the kingdom.

Salome smiles grimly.

I don't know why they listened to me at all. . . . When I finally spoke to Jesus about them, he made it clear that we really didn't understand his kingdom. Jesus asked James and John if they would be able to drink the same cup he was going to drink and they assured him they could.

Now I see what he was talking about. The cup is the one that Jesus drank yesterday.

He told them that they would drink that cup. Perhaps they, and we, will all drink that cup of death together.

Salome shakes her head.

Some of you remember that day. There was an argument when the others heard. I'll never forget what Jesus said. He talked about the fact that powerful people love hierarchy, like the Roman emperor and the high-ranking soldiers. People love to lord it over others—and I knew that he meant everyone—religious leaders over peasants, husbands over wives, rabbis over their followers. . . .

The new community would be different, Jesus said. No wonder they killed him. He said that the one who would be great must be the servant. That the one who would be first must be the slave of all. He said his own purpose was to serve and . . . to give his life for us.

Salome looks around the faces of the women.

I asked for forgiveness that day. But until yesterday, I couldn't let go. I needed to control my children, my life. I'd never given myself to Jesus. It was only at the cross that I began to see what it might mean to be abandoned to Jesus. Like my own sons, like Peter, I didn't see that his life meant his death.

By the time I saw it, he was dead. I'd never followed him.

Salome begins to cry, not a silent, controlled weeping, but the keening of one who has lost something forever. Martha pulls Salome's head onto her shoulder. Salome has not allowed another to comfort her for years, perhaps since her husband died. Her sobbing becomes a wail and then dies into a whimper.

In the silence there is a sadness, an emptiness. Regret. It is now pitch dark outside, and the loss, the finality—it overwhelms them.

The light of our lives, extinguished . . . how could life himself be never walking, talking, laughing with us?

Lydia nods.

The shepherd killed and all of us like sheep running around, not knowing where to go or what to do. The true vine cut down and the whole vineyard laid waste. All that I can think of is that we're left in a world where sin does indeed conquer good, and darkness wins over light, and the people who make rules to stay in power are vindicated in the end.

But Joanna shakes her head.

This, for us, is not a surprise. Salome, you came to Jerusalem to be with him when he died. All of us knew. Some of us saw more clearly than others that his teaching and living would lead to his death.

FIVE

Joanna looks at Jesus' mother.

The women are all afraid to ask. His mother.

When did you know he would die?

Mary. Down the centuries you have been placed on a pedestal—inaccessible—so holy, so passive, so meek. What choices did you ever have? In the paintings and sculptures, you hardly look at your baby, so distracted are you by your own holiness. Looking at your right foot, you are offered to us as a plastic model who never had any ideas, any aspirations of your own—the ideal of a good woman. You are the perfect mother, ideally sublimated to the needs of your husband and children.

No.

Not perfect. Not passive. Awful, dreadful choices.

She straightens where she sits and looks around at all the faces.

The pain of giving up my son has lasted all these years. Sometimes I found I could trust God; other times I felt overwhelmed by my fear for Jesus and my desire to protect him.

Perhaps it came to me when he preached at Nazareth.[37] It should have been a wonderful occasion. Everyone was pleased that Joseph and Mary's boy, who had practiced his carpentry craft in Nazareth, had come to preach in our synagogue. I think they all expected a fine, inspiring message.

The synagogue was full. They handed Jesus the scroll.

He unrolled it and found, quite deliberately, the Messianic prophecy of Isaiah: "The Spirit of the Lord is upon me, because he has anointed me to bring good news to the poor. He has sent me to proclaim release to the captives and recovery of sight to the blind, to let the oppressed go free, to proclaim the year of the Lord's favor." Jesus read it beautifully, and you could have heard a pin drop. Then he carefully rolled up the scroll and handed it back to the attendant and sat down. All around I felt people staring at him. What would Jesus say about this wonderful passage? What would he tell us about the glorious days that Isaiah foretold, the days that might come when their great, great, great grandchildren were grown and the Messiah would visit them and applaud them?

Jesus sat and looked at the people until the silence became uncomfortable. Finally he spoke. "Today this scripture has been fulfilled in your hearing." My heart seemed to stop, but it was as if the others didn't hear him. I heard murmurs all around me:

"What a wonderful speaker he is."

"I could listen to him read the scriptures all day."

"This is Joseph's son, isn't it?"

"Not bad for a carpenter's son."

"I always knew that boy had potential, ever since he did that chair for me. . . ."

"Have you heard about the healings he's done in Capernaum—wonderful I've heard. . . ."

I breathed a deep sigh of relief and tears of gratitude sprang to my eyes. They had missed Jesus' extraordinary words. And I realized that I was glad they had. I knew that if they heard his message, they would never sit and smile at him and damn him with such faint praise. Please, Jesus, let well enough alone. Don't say anything else.

But when did Jesus ever leave well enough alone? He told them that he guessed that they would want him to do some miracles in Nazareth, like they had heard he had done in Capernaum. "You'd probably have trouble recognizing a miracle," he said, "because this is my hometown. But that's not a new problem for the people of Israel." People were still nodding and listening. "Think of how often God has had to use foreigners because his people wouldn't cooperate with him." He mentioned Elijah and the widow at Zarephath and Naman the Syrian.

They began to hear him. I could hardly bear it. You know how people regard foreigners these days . . . people started to mutter, and their anger turned to rage about getting him out of the synagogue and out of town. The gathering began to change into a riot. A mob chased him to the edge of town.

I walked home alone slowly. I felt lonely, my life stretching before me like a nightmare. This child, this amazing son, who refused to accept superficial praise, who insisted on saying the tactless words and making sure everyone understood them. Gradually they would kill him. It seemed to me overwhelming that I should have said "yes" to having such a child.

Jesus' mother shakes her head.

I knew he would die. And so did all of you.

⚘

Mary Magdalene looks around the women's faces.[38]

I knew. From the day we visited the little town of Nain.

It was a wonderful spring day—and Nain is nestled in the hills—it looked like a little jewel. We turned off the main road and walked up toward the village.

We heard the wails of a funeral procession as we entered the town. The mourners wept loudly, and it awoke in my heart memories of my mother's funeral. Then came the bier being carried by six men—and I could hardly look at it. When I raised my eyes, there was a lovely young man with dark curls and the beginnings of a mustache. Behind swayed his mother, exhausted in her grief, her face pulled tight and pale. Someone in the crowd picked up the cry, "And she is a widow and had only this son." The woman's face collapsed. Her devastation was dreadful, and I remember thinking that she had not even realized that beyond her desperate loneliness she would face devastating poverty.

By now we were alongside the procession.

And it seemed like on this lovely spring day, the veneer of beauty had been pulled back. This young man's death and his mother's devastation were the reality, blotting out the sunshine, silencing the birds as if their heads had been twisted off.

This, I thought, is why the rulers of the synagogue always wear hard expressions at a funeral. They don't want anyone to ask where God is. They would brush a widow like this aside as a hysterical woman.

What would Jesus do?

Jesus moved to face the mother of the young man. He looked at her and shook his head as if he were deeply moved by her pain. He spoke to her.

She stood paralyzed, unable to meet Jesus' eyes. The whole crowd seemed to freeze, stuck in a moment outside time. My stomach felt chilled, though I wasn't sure why.

Only Jesus moved through the silent crowd until he was next to the bier. He reached out and touched the young man's arm and his voice split the silence. "Young man, I say to you rise." I shut my eyes, afraid to look and afraid to look away. My heart beat so loudly I thought it would break my eardrums.

How much time? Perhaps half a minute passed. And then, the boy sat bolt upright, speaking, like some people do when they've been roused from a deep sleep. The crowd stood as if they were seeing a ghost. Jesus helped the boy off the bier, as if it were the most natural thing in the world. He held his arm across the young man's back as he walked him the few steps to his mother.

Then someone broke the silence. "God has visited us!" Someone else shouted, "A prophet, a prophet."

My eyes were on the woman. "My son!" she cried and tears poured down her face. They clung to each other and then the son laughed, a rich, hearty laugh for one so young. Jesus watched them and laughed, too.

For several minutes there is a silence, some of the women imagining, some of them remembering. One whispers what they all must be thinking: "How could one who brought the dead to life . . . ?" Mary Magdalene shakes her head.

It was as if this pretty little town, hidden in the hills, had gotten more than it bargained for, more than it dreamed of. Nain was too small, too insignificant to contain the glory. The boy hadn't asked to be pulled back from death. His mother would not have dared to ask. Jesus' ministry was out of the bounds of decorum and reason; it was extravagant; it was dangerous.

I felt frightened for him then, a little spark of fear that I carried in my heart from that day onward.

All I'd expected was a walk on a lovely spring day; all the people of Nazareth wanted was a nice sermon.

Martha looks around at the women, and seems to force herself to sit down.[39]

I confess to you, my sisters—I didn't want Jesus to offer me more than I wanted.

The pain in Martha's face barely covers her energy and intensity. Her strength for many years had been channeled into homemaking, and she had done that with a kind of fierceness. Martha was the kind of person who would know, only too well, that women don't listen to rabbis. She wouldn't want to raise difficult issues. To question a woman's life and possibilities would free monsters, deep in her psyche, dreaded questions about how a woman might invest her days, about how she had used her life.

We were fortunate to see Jesus often. We realized, after hearing him teach near the temple, that he would need a place to stay when he visited Jerusalem and we invited him to make Bethany his second home.

I've always been known for my cooking, my dinner parties, for managing the servants. I knew that Jesus would find Bethany refreshing.

The competition between Martha and her sister Maria must have flared from mild to intense. Reserved Maria, who seldom spoke her thoughts or feelings, might have seen Martha's attention to detail as shallow and trivial. The seven days of menstruation each month—when Martha couldn't prepare food without making it unclean—must have been a trial for both of them as Maria tried to manage the meals and Martha offered tidbits of annoying advice.

Martha hesitates, afraid to make her confession, although it is perhaps the most common admission that a woman could make. But it's not something women talk about much—the fact that the

*judgments made on their cooking, housekeeping, and entertaining,
seem somehow like a judgment of their souls. That the way they
make a holiday successful for the family looms larger than the last
trump. Martha takes a deep breath, and then speaks.*

Each time Jesus came I wanted to refresh and impress
him a little more. I'd add another course, a new fruit drink.
He'd say, "This lemon juice is lovely and refreshing,
Martha. Thank you very much."

I loved doing that for the teacher. But the satisfaction
didn't last a minute; it never filled me up. I felt a thrill, just
as I did when someone told me I was a great cook, a good
baker, a wonderful hostess—but then it was gone and of
course, I needed more.

One day, perhaps eighteen months ago, he was here. I
was in the kitchen fuming as I prepared a meal and suddenly it seemed to me that no one really appreciated all that
I was doing for them. Jesus and some of the followers from
Galilee and Maria were sitting, sitting right in this room,
and Jesus was talking to them. Why should I slave away
while they sat? Didn't they realize that what I was doing
was just as important? Seeing Maria with them really both-
ered me. She should help me prepare food, not be carried
away with theological speculations.

I marched over to them. Jesus had just finished a story
and everyone was laughing. I interrupted. "Jesus. Look at
me. I'm hot and I've been working practically single-
handedly trying to get supper, and Maria is sitting here
taking her ease. Tell her to give me a hand, or we'll never
get our meal."

I wouldn't have been surprised if the others had laughed. But before anyone else could say a word or Maria could stand up, Jesus spoke.

He looked at me with urgent concern. "Martha, Martha." His voice echoes in my mind even now. "You are so worried and distracted by many things; there is need of only one thing. Maria has chosen the better part, which shall not be taken away from her."

When I spoke to Jesus, I expected a quick solution. I thought he would tell Maria to help me. I should have known him better. He knew this was no minor issue; in fact, it touched the heart of who I was, how I was spending my life, what made me feel worthwhile. It touched the center of my relationship with God.

I felt dizzy, almost winded, so I sat down. Jesus turned to finish answering a question. I don't remember what he said, but I realized that I could sit there, too. I could ask questions and wonder and ponder and learn. I could choose the better part.

The world would go on if we had a simple meal. And I would learn to survive without compliments to feed me, without frantic efforts to prove myself. I sat, feeling weak and light-headed, with the weight that had been removed from me. I could just be, in the presence of the teacher.

How many women have missed God's visitation—have swept him out of the kitchen because he was distracting them?[40]

How wonderful that Luke included this story in his gospel. It's easy to get the impression that only the weighty doctrinal matters captured Jesus' attention. He understood the pressures women face to perform, and he (and Luke) took this incident seriously. Jesus' call to Martha, to Maria, to all women is to put their discipleship first.

The lentils burned that day . . . we laughed about it. And when Maria and I talked afterward, I felt so stupid that I'd been trying to impress the Messiah with my culinary skills!

Martha shakes her head.

When I'm upset, as I have been the last few days, there's a part of me that wants to organize meals, spring clean the house. . . .

I cannot say how deeply I regret those minutes, hours, days, which I wasted cooking this and that, while I could have been sitting with Jesus. I guess that we never realize that we may not have all the time in the world to do what is really important.

It is after midnight. Martha stands and moves into the kitchen. A few minutes later she brings a basket of bread in the room. She kneels on the mat and hands chunks of it to the women. Miriam hands a piece to Jesus' mother. She shakes her head, and sighs.

He asked us to give up what was most precious. . . .

Earlier today I found myself longing for Elizabeth.[41]
And although I have missed her very deeply since she died,
I am glad that she does not face this.

Perhaps if I had learned more from Elizabeth's pain in
giving up her son, these last months would not have been
so hard.

Elizabeth had no large dreams: she only asked for a small
house and children. After her marriage to Zechariah, her
monthly disappointments grew from small twinges of pain
to an obsession: she could not look at a baby, so great was
her longing. Twenty gnawing years went by. She told me,
and I almost a child at the time, that she suspected that God
had judged her for some unknown sin. She became super-
stitious, promising God she would do anything to atone, if
only God would give her a child.

But Elizabeth, even when Jesus and John were small,
saw it clearly: that part of all motherhood is the sacrifice of
the child.[42] She knew that John was unusual, and struggled
with her fantasies that he would meet a nice girl in the
village who would put up with his foibles and that he
would settle in a little house and make a fine father in a
distracted sort of way.

And then John began his ministry. He spoke the truth
—exactly what people needed to hear, Elizabeth told me,
with pride and fear in her voice. Not many months later I

heard Herod had put John in prison. Elizabeth was frantic about John, and it hurt her to hear people talk endlessly about Jesus.

When Herod had John beheaded, Elizabeth took it very hard. Most women know what it is to lose a child, but Elizabeth had offered this precious child to God; she felt he had been used up and then dumped, stuck in prison to suffer a hideous death.

We see Mary in the Pieta. She sits with the body of her lifeless son across her lap, she is appalled by his death.

I found giving up my child no easier than Elizabeth did.

But first Mary was appalled by his life, by his demands that she be more than his mother.[43] Why has this been overlooked?

It was several months after Jesus spoke at Nazareth before I felt strong enough to go with a few friends to hear Jesus teach in Capernaum. When we got there the house was so crowded that I couldn't even see him. Someone in the crowd recognized me, and asked if I was his mother. Yes, I nodded, I am his mother. People whispered and began to clear a way for me to get inside. Someone shouted to Jesus that his mother was waiting to see him.

Jesus didn't even look at me. He looked around the crowd and told a group of strangers that they were his family. He said that those who do God's will were his mother and sisters and brothers.

My face began to burn. I felt embarrassed, angry. Washing his clothes, cooking for him, rocking him all those nights when he was sick, defending him from the taunts of other children: to Jesus they were nothing. . . .

Mary. To give your life wholly for the life of the child: your culture and so many after honored this as the highest calling of women. But he threw that back at you, stripped you of that way of finding, peeled off that way of knowing who you were. You must have felt dizzy, knocked off balance.

Why did he insist on taking away all that I had? Like Elizabeth, I felt that I asked for so little and he wouldn't even leave me with that. . . .

Two weeks later I was still licking my wounds. I hoped Jesus would come and visit. I did not expect him to apologize—just to come for a visit. But instead one evening Joseph came home from hearing Jesus teach. "Mary," he said. "I need to tell you something." Jesus had been speaking in Capernaum and a woman had called to him, "Blessed are the breasts you sucked and the womb that bore you!"

My heart beat faster. We've all heard that accolade of the mother of a special person. My face must have shown my hope. Joseph shook his head sorrowfully. He said he wanted to tell me so that I didn't hear it from someone else. Jesus corrected the woman sharply, telling her that blessed rather are those who follow him and are committed to the Kingdom of God.

Mary shakes her head. She could just manage the pain of this extraordinary son, as long as she could slip quietly into the role of mother, as long as she was honored for that. Many women know that feeling only too well. It feels frightening, traumatic, to be pushed to find meaning outside those relationships in which they've invested themselves. Valued as wombs and breasts, as mothers and nurturers. Mary covers her face with her hands.

To relinquish that special place: that was hardest. I can't say how many months of sleepless nights I endured before I understood what Jesus was saying. He was saying: "No. You are a follower of God. A friend of God." More than womb and breasts. Not less . . . more. But oh so hard to make that change.

When I saw him yesterday carrying his cross to Golgotha, I realized that the weight he carried and the weight that I have carried—all those years since I said "yes" to the heavenly presence—these were all one. The burden of bearing and raising him, of fearing for him and wishing he would please rather than upset people. The terrible risk of letting go, of becoming more than mother. As he walked toward his death bearing his gallows on his back, I saw that I was complicit in his death: that we chose it together. I by saying "yes" to God, he by being true to his message. "Walk on, my son, walk on . . ." I said to him. I let him go again.

Each woman sits in her own world of sorrow and loss. Pondering her own yes to Jesus, and what that has meant, afraid to even contemplate what it might mean, his mother dries her eyes.

There is one more part I have not told you.

During that first visitation, when I said yes to bearing Jesus, the presence told me that Elizabeth was pregnant. God could never have given me a more wonderful gift than those three months. Elizabeth and I talked about God's goodness and our babies soon to be born, while Zechariah moved silently around the house.

That first day, just after I walked into Elizabeth's home, God seemed to speak to me about what Jesus' birth and life would mean. I remember it still.[44]

Standing there with Elizabeth, it seemed clear to me that the wonder of God was revealed in his visiting someone like me. I knew that others would look at me and see me as fortunate because of what God had done. I knew of his faithfulness to his faithful people. . . .

She hesitates, and then continues.

I am not sure who would call me fortunate today. It is true that God's faithfulness seemed so clear then, and has often since, but . . .

That day I felt he was saying that God, in sending the Messiah was scattering the proud from their proud thinking, and bringing down the powerful from their power. And it has seemed like that. That he would lift up the lowly and fill the hungry with good things, while those who were rich would be sent away.

Now I do not know what to think of those words. I've carried them with me all these years.

Six

The words of Jesus' mother have stirred the women. They have never heard them before, and they seem like words to hang onto, words that bring sense to the chaos of the last few weeks. As they sit, a lamp splutters out. Mary Magdalene speaks.

Mary. We've spent much of the day and now long into the night talking about the way he lifted us—the lowliest of society—the way he lifted us up. And the proud—he scattered them and showed them they weren't so wonderful as they thought.

Mary Magdalene wants them to see what is clear to her: that Jesus' teaching this last week all makes sense when you hear the words given to his mother so long ago. Although all these women were at the cross, many were not with him when he confronted the religious leaders in Jerusalem during what has come to be called Holy Week. She trembles as she speaks.

This last week all his teaching has been pointed at the proud and powerful.[45] He told them that they cleaned only the outside of their cups and left the inside filthy. He called them fools, who tithed all their little herbs, but neglected the justice and the love of God. It made him furious that the teachers loaded people with heavy burdens and never lifted even a tiny finger to help them carry the weight. He shouted at them for stealing the key of knowledge from the people who needed it. He said they didn't bother to enter God's kingdom and blocked others out too. Jesus thundered at them that they had always killed the prophets and were getting ready to do it again. He told them that the tax collectors and prophets were getting into the kingdom of God ahead of them.[46]

When I was little, my father told me that the great difference between our faith and that of the pagans was practice. The pagans simply had to believe but we were called to live out our faith, even when our belief waned. But Jesus spoke of the danger of this—how the living heart of religion could atrophy and the practice go on and on and on . . . until the center was irretrievably lost.

Jesus did exactly what you said, Mary. He lifted up the helpless and scattered the proud. There was one day last week when the teachers tried to catch him out, reminding him that the law of Moses commanded the stoning of a woman caught in the act of adultery.[47] They brought this poor woman and threw her on the ground in front of him, gloating, staring at her as she tried to cover her nakedness. Jesus wouldn't look at her while they were there. He drew in the dust and then spoke, quietly, asking the one who hadn't sinned to start throwing stones. The silence was stunning. None of them could do it. Only after the teachers had gone did Jesus look at the woman. "Where are they?" "Gone," she said. "I don't condemn you," Jesus said to her. "Go and sin no more."

I loved Jesus for that, but I also felt terribly afraid. I looked in those teachers' eyes and I saw fear. When the powerful are afraid then the weak should tremble. Nothing will stop the powerful who feel threatened. I knew that. I could see their fear hardening into bitterness and hatred, and there could be no going back.

The first day of last week, I hoped—only for a few hours—
that my foreboding was wrong. I had known Jesus as meaning, as love and as friend, and as the promised one of God,
and suddenly it seemed that all of Jerusalem recognized
their rescuer.[48]

There was Jesus riding on a colt—just like the prophet
had predicted of the Christ—and all of us followers and
thousands of others had lined the streets shouting and wav-
ing branches and spreading their cloaks for his colt. I
walked a few feet from him, shouting when I could, but
most of the time I couldn't speak.

"Hosanna!"

"Blessed is the one who comes in the Name of the
Lord!"

"Peace in heaven and glory in the highest!"

I wept. My worst fears were swept away—now Jesus
could begin his new community, finally proclaimed as the
Messiah.

Then I looked at the Pharisees. They stood with faces
like death. Two of them pushed through the crowd to Jesus.
"Teacher," one said, shock and fury contorting his face.
"Order your disciples to stop. You can't let them do this."

Jesus looked at them. "I tell you, if these people were
silent all these stones around you would shout." They
turned away, livid. Jesus was putting down the mighty from
their seats. I was trembling.

We walked further to that point where you get a wonderful view of the city.[49] Jesus stopped, and we watched

him, wondering what he would do or say. To our surprise, he began to weep. Judas was standing behind me and he started muttering. "What does he want? Finally they're cheering for him, they're going to make him King. What kind of moment is this to show weakness?"

Jesus began to speak to the city. "If you had only recognized on this day the things that make for peace! But now they are hidden from your eyes." Then his eyes seemed distant, as if another time had pushed that moment out of the way. He started to talk about enemies around the city and people being crushed and no stone left on another . . . it was horrible, and all this would happen, because people refused to recognize the fact that they had been visited by God. My heart felt like it had turned to ice. What was Jesus saying? Then someone took up the shouting again and we walked on.

After that the conflict only became more intense.[50] When we walked into the temple courtyard, the sight of the Scribes and Pharisees and Sadducees—the powerful— while the poor and wretched were being cheated by the money changers . . . I've seen him angry before—we all have, when he sees a helpless person mistreated. But I'd never seen his fury. The looks on the faces of those money changers as Jesus turned over their tables, and they scrambled after their coins and ran for the gates . . . Jesus thundered: "It is written, 'My house shall be a house of prayer'; but you have made it a den of robbers." The religious leaders watched, eyes burning with hatred.

Then the endless arguments.[51] One religious leader after another interrupted him asking questions—each one so difficult that a murmur of dismay went through the crowd. They just wanted to hear Jesus teach. How could he answer such a question without getting into trouble? "Which is the greatest commandment?" "What authority do you teach by?" "Should we pay taxes to Caesar?" "If a woman had seven husbands which would be her husband in the resurrection?" "Who is David's son?" Jesus answered them all.

Jesus was so brilliant in all his answers; the crowd cheered wildly. "That's telling him, Jesus. All right." But he wouldn't leave the authorities alone. Over and over I wanted to shout, "Jesus, stop. You don't need to set the whole world straight. Leave them. . . ." He told them they were in trouble because they didn't practice what they preached and they liked to be seen and praised by people and get the best places at the synagogues and be greeted in the markets. He told them they devoured widows' homes and that their prayers were long and empty and that they carefully kept picky rules and forgot about justice and mercy. That the one who got it right was the poor widow[52] who pleased God by giving from her heart. The crowds cheered and the Pharisees got colder and more sullen at each word.

John told me once that when the Pharisees started their movement it was to make the faith more pure and holy. But somehow they'd lost that when they came to power; they couldn't let go of their positions; they couldn't open their hands to give or receive. I realized as I looked at them and listened to their arguing that that's what's wrong with us—I mean as human beings—the heart of our sin is that we begin to pay attention to little details and codify them and sanctify them until they are all we remember. We love trifles because we can control them. We forget the heart of faith and life and love and truth, which we can't control. It frightened me to think that even the message of Jesus might someday be turned into a religious poison and used against people.

The arguments began to ring in my head. Over and over I remembered Jesus' words that he had to go to Jerusalem because that's where the prophets were killed. And we were in Jerusalem.

Finally Jesus spoke the words that seemed to spell his death: "Do you see these great buildings?" he asked, pointing to the temple.[53] How could you miss them—golden in the afternoon sunlight—standing as if they'd been there forever and would be there until the end of the world. "There will not be left one stone upon another that will not be thrown down." The religious leaders looked at each other. At that moment I felt in their eyes that the end had come. Jesus went on teaching about signs of the end of the world. He was right: my world was ending. It was as if he were getting further and further away until I could hardly hear him. The sun seemed dark and cold even as he spoke. I needed to try to do something—anything—to keep them from killing Jesus. I couldn't listen anymore—I had to get away.

Mary Magdalene runs out of steam. She had begun her story of the last week full of excitement about the way the words of Jesus' mother fit with his life. But now the terror, the fear, the conflict,

the powerlessness of those last days in Jerusalem overwhelm her.
She falls onto her knees, weeping.

And now, it's happened. What will God do to us? Not only
have we killed the prophets but now the rescuer, the Christ
of God.[54]

Joanna speaks:

We've all asked the question, "How could he die?"
But maybe the real question is "How could good have lived
this long in this world?"

Salome looks around the women, her voice desperate.

Watching at the cross—people coming up and seeing
his agony and laughing, shouting to him, "Hey I thought
you were supposed to be such big stuff?!"

"So if you can be so helpful to other people, why
don't you help yourself?"

"Where's your power now, big boy?!"

"Here's your great opportunity to show us that you're
the Messiah—hop down from the cross!"

Or watching as the soldiers nailed him to the cross
. . . helpless and powerless as they tortured him. When
they jolted his cross into the ground, one of them laughed,
"Now you'll feel it, King!"

Mary Magdalene covers her face.

Three hours . . . three years . . . three lifetimes. . . . Did the sky really turn black, or were my eyes unable to stand any more pain . . . they darkened themselves? Maybe sunshine can never be the same again. . . .

My world gone sunless . . . and his voice screaming through it: "My God, my God, why have you forsaken me?"

The minutes stretch out. The house is cold, in that coldest hour of the night. Mary Magdalene shakes her head.

At the cross, John kept sobbing that they were all scared, and somehow they hadn't realized that Jesus was going to die. John felt like he'd lost his chance to be the friend Jesus needed.

John told me about their Passover meal. . . . Jesus had washed their dirty feet and told them they would eat his body and drink his blood and find life. We stood there below that cross, seeing his torn flesh, his blood dripping down, and the life being sapped out of him. . . .

Mary's sobs fade into quiet weeping. It's a wonderful sentiment, and it's all supposed to fit, but somehow. . . . And it does fit. What Jesus did made him a dangerous radical, a revolutionary. He had to be killed. But how could the Christ die?

Joanna speaks again.

We all knew that the new wine would never fit. We wanted to believe that the Messiah must be victorious. But he said that a grain of wheat had to fall into the ground and die, or it would live alone. That the greatest would be the least.

Rhoda breaks her long silence.

We've known. We all knew that we needed to make this final journey together. To be with him as he died.

Lydia also must speak.

We knew because our own stories, of our own worlds tipped upside down, have all really been part of the big story.

Joanna nods.

It all fits. God chooses the Messiah to be born in a humble town of humble parents. To join this new community even the great teachers must be reborn and become like children. The poor, the humble and the meek find life —the rich, the proud, and the self-satisfied lose all. It is the great reversal: the teacher washes the feet of the followers.

Mary Magdalene turns, her face still wet, her hair tangled. She pushes her hair back and twists it.

It's terribly important. What were the words God gave you, even while Jesus' life was stirring within you?

Jesus' mother recites the words again.

He has filled the hungry with good things, but the rich have been sent away empty. He has put down the mighty from their seats, and exalted the humble and meek.

Mary Magdalene nods. She wants to remember these words to tell herself in the days that are coming, the days which will be worse than today, the days that will wrench away all belief. . . .

Maria, sister of Martha, moves forward into the circle so that the lamplight falls on her. Maria is a person of few words and she has spoken little in this circle. She is the kind of person who is afraid to trust herself to others for fear she will lose them.

It is my turn to speak.

Now, at the darkest hour of the night, Maria begins to tell her story.[55]

Jesus stayed with us several times a year. When he visited, deep inside I felt myself blossoming, growing in understanding and faith. Because we looked after him, I think I believed that he belonged to us. Perhaps we all feel that. I felt I loved him as much as I had ever loved anyone.

A year ago Jesus left us after a festival to go across the Jordan River. He had only been gone a few days when Lazarus became sick. We waited a night and a day, thinking he would get better, but instead his fever got higher and he developed a terrible cough and started hallucinating. He talked to mother and father as if they were still alive.

I told Martha that I was scared. I thought he was going to die. Did she think we should call Jesus? She agreed and so we sent one of the men from the village to find him and tell him that Lazarus was sick, and could he come quickly.

We knew he would have no trouble finding Jesus. You know how word about Jesus' travels and where he could be found flew around any area.

We waited. Waiting: the suns seems to crawl up the sky, hang above you, and then creep down the other side. And the night is eternal . . . I felt myself pulling back inside, like an animal withdrawing into its hole to hibernate, pulling in, trying to slow down my heart-beat so that the passage of time would not hurt so much.

The man from the village came back the next day and told us that he had given Jesus the message. "Did he say anything?" Martha asked. He shook his head. "Didn't seem to be in a particular hurry."

Martha reported this to me while I was sitting with Lazarus. He was raving, clearly suffering, and I felt as if I had been slapped. Jesus loved Lazarus. He loved Martha and he loved me. How could he act as if there were no hurry?

Lazarus groaned and wailed.

"If Jesus were here . . ." Martha said. "Maybe he

knows that Lazarus is just about to get better . . . or maybe he will just pray and Lazarus will be better. . . . don't you remember John telling us about that centurion whose servant was healed?"

"Martha, Lazarus is not getting better. He is dying."

She lowered herself down next to me. Lazarus rolled and lashed out in all directions, shrieking, for an hour or more. Then he drew a deep breath and fell back, silent.

We sat for—I don't know how long it was—neither of us speaking. Our little brother. . . . Then one of the servants came in . . . looked at us and started to cry. Martha spoke, perhaps to the servant, or to no one in particular. "If Jesus had been here, Lazarus would not have died."

I could not speak. Was it worse that Lazarus was dead, or that Jesus hadn't come? What had made me think that Jesus loved us?

We all know too well the blur of those few days after a death: getting a body ready for burial, preparing spices. The tomb was ready and we laid him in it and the local rabbi read from the Torah. People from Jerusalem heard of his death and came out to mourn with us—the house seemed full, jammed with people wailing and mourning. I couldn't explain to them why my eyes were dry. For Lazarus I might have wept, but for my deeper desolation . . .

Every time a new group came toward the house, I looked up, heart pounding, hoping it was Jesus; hoping it wasn't. He didn't come. With each disappointment a part of my heart seemed to be frozen off, until only a tiny bit was left beating. How could he not come? Over and over I told myself: Jesus may be a great miracle worker, and everyone knows he is an extraordinary teacher, but all the talk of love. . . . Too cozy. Who did I think I was?

Martha kept saying, "If Jesus had been here, Lazarus wouldn't have died." I wanted to shriek at her—"Yes but he wasn't here, dammit. He doesn't care. Stop babbling like a fool." I was silent.

Embarrassed by the strength of her emotion, Maria breaks off. Martha fills the silence.

I was more confused than angry. It seemed to me that there must have been some mistake. Or he had a good reason for his delay. I guess I said that over and over to try to convince myself. Then one of the servants came in—my sister and I were in the kitchen—and said that Jesus was coming. Maria shook her head and sat where she was. I dropped the onions from my apron and ran out to meet him on the road, down by the bend coming from Jerusalem. When I saw him I stopped and I looked at him: "Lord if you had been here, my brother would not have died . . . and even now . . ."

Jesus took my hand and said to me that my brother would rise again and I said, "Of course, I know that he will rise again in the resurrection on the last day." I was parroting the truth[56] I'd learned from childhood. I knew that it wasn't as if I'd never see Lazarus again.

But Jesus stopped me. He said, "I am the resurrection and the life. Those who believe in me, even though they die, will live, and everyone who believes in me will never die."

Martha's eyes fill with tears as she looks around the circle.

Everyone who believes in me will never die. That's what he said. He asked me if I believed that. And it seemed to me that I was being asked to make an enormous leap, from believing that something might happen someday, to seeing Jesus as life and resurrection—as life which could never be stopped, never be put out. It all seemed to click together.

I said to him, "Yes, Lord, I believe that you are the Messiah, the Son of God, the one coming into the world." It all seemed so clear. . . .

How these words about life and death sound to these women as the last hours of this night run out: somehow they had gotten it all wrong. Martha cries, almost as if she's said something blasphemous.

How could I have been so mistaken?

She gulps a few breaths and then goes on with her story.

And then he smiled at me, almost as if I'd been a very good student, and said that I should call Maria. So I ran, and there she was still in the kitchen with the other women, and I whispered to her that Jesus was here and he was calling her.

Maria, her look far off as she remembers, pulls her tunic around her and speaks.

I didn't want to see him at all. If I had to, I wanted to be alone. But of course the other mourners thought I was going to the tomb and leapt up to come with me. I'd never felt such a range of emotions. I felt annoyed by all the people around, devastated by the loss of my little brother. And furious with Jesus for not coming when we needed him—I just wanted to damn well be left alone to lick my wounds.

And I resented the fact that when I saw Jesus, he would see me so clearly that he would understand all I was feeling. Could I keep nothing as my very own? My brother was gone, my trust in a friend shattered—couldn't I have some privacy even over my own soul, for God's sake?!

Minutes or hours later I reached him. I couldn't look into his face, so I knelt in front of him. My body was kneeling, but my heart was defiant, raging so that I was beyond words. I won't tell you what I wanted to say. As the other mourners straggled up to us, I had to say something. All I could think of was what Martha had been parroting for four days, "Lord if you had been here, my brother would not have died."

Even as I said it I knew it sounded as if I were prattling a nursery rhyme. I knew that Jesus understood my anger and pain and my terrible sense of loss. I wanted to be strong, to keep all the walls I had built around my heart, to not contemplate the possibility that God loved me, that Jesus could be trusted. My tears overflowed. I couldn't hide from him.

And when I looked up into his face, I didn't want to.

I saw that he understood.

No. More than understood. His eyes . . . there was a look in them that I'd never seen. Jesus looked deeply, profoundly disturbed. Angry. My rage paled beside this emotion of his. He made a terrible sound, something between a groan and a sigh. The mourners had taken up their wailing, but this sound came from so deep inside Jesus, that their wails sounded trivial. Pain like the deepest wound in the heart of God.

"Where is he?" Jesus asked.

I was still in front of Jesus. He took my arm and gently pulled me up. "Where have they put him?"

"Right this way. . . . Come on over here. . . ." the others were saying. We all walked toward the tomb.

We got there, and the tears washed over me afresh. How could someone so young and full of fun and vitality—how could he be dead in there? It didn't fit—the world was all wrong: broken, warped, cracked. We stood in the sunshine with bright flowers climbing, sprawling. Light and fragrance seemed like an insult, a sick joke—next to the darkness, the chill, the finality of death.

I struggled to turn my thoughts into words. How could the world be like this? I turned to Jesus. His cheeks were as wet as mine, his tears freely flowing as he looked toward the stone.

The other mourners were touched. They said things like, "Jesus really loved Lazarus, didn't he?" and "He's made the blind to see, you would have thought that he could've done something to keep Lazarus from dying of the fever."

But as I watched him, it seemed to me that I understood. I saw that Jesus' tears were not for Lazarus only, but for more. He was weeping not only for the loss of his friend, or for my pain, but for the way the world is bent and disjointed . . . people lose hope, children die, friends are pulled apart, the poor starve, evil triumphs. . . .

And again Jesus groaned, with a sound that seemed to carry all the pain of a world gone wrong. My stomach turned over. . . .

"Take away the stone." I was so distraught that I hardly knew what he was saying. Martha grimaced and took Jesus' arm: "Lord, there is already a smell. Don't forget he's been dead four days." He looked at her, almost as if she weren't there and told her she would see God's glory.

Martha gestured, trembling, to some of the men and they came out of the crowd and heaved away at the stone. We watched, breathless. The mourners had stopped their wailing. The silence was eerie.

The tears still ran down my face and my heart pounded so that I could hardly hear Jesus praying, asking God to hear him.

Then his voice seemed to shake the trees: "Lazarus, come out!" We stood. I found Martha's hand and clutched it tight. The silence was deafening. Then we heard a small rustle and some jostling around inside the tomb, and . . . out he came, looking very odd in the bandages and his eyes blinking in the sun. Clearly, he couldn't remember what had happened and why he was wearing this get up. Martha and I ran to him and started to unwrap the cloths—has anyone ever had a more joyful task?

We laughed and cried, and teased him about wearing such difficult clothing, and he gradually figured out what was going on, though he was dazed, and seemed to find it hard to talk afterward about the whole experience. Said he'd seen wonderful things . . .

The women sit in silence. Finally Maria speaks again, her voice shaking.

This will sound very strange to you, but since that afternoon I've known that Jesus would die.

Since I saw Jesus at Lazarus' tomb. Saw his pain interwoven with my pain. Saw his tears in the face of separation and death . . .

We've all said that his message was too new—that it would burst the wineskins, that people would want to kill him. I'm sure that is part of it. But his ministry—amazing as it was—it was not deep enough.

Raising one dead person . . . or even three or four . . . it was wonderful but it didn't reach the heart of the problem . . . pain . . . alienation . . . death itself.

The heart of Jesus could never stand outside looking in. His way was to get into the middle . . . of the pain and the fear . . . to become one with it . . . and to shine his light from the inside out.

He had to go into the middle of death itself. It fit completely with who Jesus was, with the rest of his life. Never aloof, never apart from, always within, always closer than close.

He had to do it. I knew he would die. Beyond a shadow of a doubt . . .

Maria stares. She can't look at the others.

He didn't understand death's finality.

She shakes her head, and just manages to get the words out.

That when he died there would be no one left to raise him.

The silence stretches and circles the room. Finally Mary Magdalene speaks.

That's why you brought the perfume that night.

Maria speaks between her sobs.[57]

What else could I do? I knew he was going to die. I wanted to show him, before it was too late, how much I loved him.

I took all the money I had ever had, all that had come to me through father's death. I'd never held so much money in my life. I went into Jerusalem and bought the nard—it was in a lovely jar made of alabaster—the most beautiful thing I'd ever seen.

It was made to be broken . . . the sheer excessiveness and luxury . . . of beauty designed to be shattered . . . it nearly overwhelmed me as I carried the jar back to Bethany.

When I walked into the room bearing this miracle of outrageous extravagance, there was some theological discussion going on. Jesus looked exhausted and preoccupied. I stood beside him. I took that beautiful jar and hit it on the stone floor and the neck of it broke right off. Then I poured the ointment on Jesus' head. The fragrance of the perfume filled the house, and for a moment I was outside time—Jesus and I together. We only were there—my love and I. I expressing my adoration.

He looked at me in that moment, and I could see he knew he would die. That he knew I knew. That it was excruciating for him. I knelt down and poured the last of the ointment on his lovely feet, and wiped them with my hair. . . .

I don't know how long Jesus and I were outside time.

I began to hear a voice. Judas grumbling about money for the poor. He didn't understand.

But Jesus understood. He said that he was only with us for a little while, and that I was anointing his body for burial.

Maria looks at the floor. She cannot speak. But Martha also was there. She tells the others what Jesus said.

He said, Maria, that when the story was told, his story, that what you did would be told in memory of you.

Maria shakes her head.

I don't understand that.

She wants nothing that will separate her from her sisters.

I don't need to. It was enough . . . to tell him how much I loved him. . . .

At this moment all the women shift as they sit, a few shaking their heads, some weeping. And then they begin to speak.

If only . . .
I wish that I had . . .

I never really told him . . .
Why didn't I . . .
I loved him . . .

Maria looks at the women, almost frightened, afraid she has broken the circle. To have missed the chance, forever, to express their love. The pain runs throughout the room, excruciating loss, tinged with jealousy. Maria speaks, her voice stronger.

No. I was only doing what we have all done. I was expressing my love, giving myself to him. . . . You have all done the same. You were all there by the cross, all with him as he died.

And you have followed him since he touched you. Those are our stories, told here today even as the sun set and as the night has run.

She looks slowly, deliberately at each woman.

Like you, Lydia, Rhoda. And you, Susannah and Joanna. Like you, Salome. And you, his own mother, when you were visited and you told the angel that you were the Lord's handmaid, and you would give yourself to him . . . Like you Mary, from the moment he delivered you.

I did the same.

The women are all silent, immersed in their own pain. They look at each other, and after a few moments, Mary Magdalene speaks.

I think I understand what Jesus meant when he said what you did will be remembered. It will be told, because what you did was the very center of Jesus' life and our life with him. The heart of the story is about those who give themselves to Jesus, as Jesus gave himself to us. We didn't fully understand, but we came to him with open hands. . . .

Maria's right . . . we've all done that. Since the day each of us began to follow him. . . . At the cross as we stood with him. . . . Tonight as our stories have made the night holy. We all wish that we'd done it by pouring out a wonderful perfume, by touching him. What wouldn't any of us give for a last chance to tell him we love him, to see his smile of love as we pour ointment on him. . . .

Mary Magdalene looks toward the window, toward the pale lightening rim at the edge of the sky.

He can't hear us. . . . He'll never smile at us again. . . .

Soon it will be dawn. She struggles to her feet.

It is late . . . probably less than an hour until the day's dawning.

Don't you see . . . even though he is dead, we can still offer ourselves to him. We can anoint his body.[58]

Mary Magdalene leans over Jesus' mother and kisses her. She looks at her deeply.

Please stay and rest for a few hours, and then the others will bring you over to the tomb when it is warmer. . . .

She moves to pick up her cloak.

I must go now, and be with him. . . .

She stands in the doorway with Salome and Miriam. The others in the circle hold back their cries of fear and longing. They will wait and follow when it is light. None of these women—so full of faith and love—know what they will find at the tomb.

Mary Magdalene stops, looks around the circle, and speaks to all the women.

Don't be afraid. We will never forget him. Love is as strong as death.

And they move into the darkness, holding spices and ointments to anoint the one they love.

Epilogue

Early on the first day of the week, while it was still dark, Mary Magdalene came to the tomb and saw that the stone had been removed from the tomb.

But Mary stood weeping outside the tomb. As she wept, she bent over to look into the tomb; and she saw two angels in white, sitting where the body of Jesus had been lying, one at the head and the other at the feet. They said to her, "Woman, why are you weeping?" She said to them, "They have taken away my Lord, and I do not know where they have laid him." When she had said this, she turned around and saw Jesus standing there, but she did not know that it was Jesus. Jesus said to her, "Woman, why are you weeping? Whom are you looking for?" Supposing him to be the gardener, she said to him, "Sir, if you have carried him away, tell me where you have laid him, and I will take him away." Jesus said to her, "Mary!" She turned and said to him in Hebrew, "Rabbouni!" (which means Teacher).[59]

—JOHN 20:1, 11–16

ENDNOTES

1. Matthew, Mark, Luke, and John give us different lists of the women who were at the cross the day before, differing probably because the audiences for whom they were writing would have known some of the women better than others. See Luke 23:49–56; Matthew 27:55–61; Mark 15:40–47; John 19:25–27.

Just the fact that all these women were here is quite remarkable. The journey from Galilee to Jerusalem was approximately a hundred miles depending on the route. For women to travel without a husband or father escorting them would have been shocking. For them to travel in a mixed group would have violated societal and religious norms. According to scholars, "following" in "all the texts is a technical term for complete participation in the conviction and activity of the traveling preachers" (Susanne Heine, *Women and Early Christianity*, Minneapolis: Augsburg, 1987, 61).

As Gerd Theissen points out in his book *The Gospels in Context* (Minneapolis: Fortress Press, 1991), the use of place names to identify characters (such as Mary Magdalene, Joseph of Arimethea, and Simon of Cyrene) makes sense because these people were out of their normal contexts. Normally people were known by the names of their fathers, who would have been unknown in Jerusalem. Thus because Mary Magdalene's father would have been unknown to people in Jerusalem she was known by her place of origin. Other women in the narratives may have been known by different names depending on the gospel writer's sense of the identification which would have worked best for his particular audience.

2. The women would have gathered at Martha and Mary's house in Bethany, which is a few miles over the Mount of Olives from the holy city. Edwin Jerome O'Connor in his book *The Holy Land* points out that most pilgrims to Jerusalem during the great festivals had a regular place to stay when the population of Jerusalem tripled. Jesus seemed to use Bethany as his regular stopping place.

The house probably had a few sleeping rooms and a courtyard, a kitchen area and a common room, with mats on the floor. See Exodus 35:2–3.

3. See John 19:38–39.

4. See Luke 23:48–56; Matthew 27:57–61; Mark 15:42–47. We have in our minds an impression from paintings of the crucifixion of Jesus' followers standing at the foot of the cross for hours on end. In fact it was very dangerous for family and friends of the crucified to be seen near a cross. Particularly if found to be mourning, they could themselves be crucified. This had happened to women and children, and certainly Jesus' followers knew this. At the cross there are a large number of Jesus' women followers, mentioned in all the gospels, and twice by Mark in both 15:40 and 15:41.

L. Schottroff argues in her article "Maria Magdalena und die Frauen am Grabe" (*Evangelische Theologie 42,* translated by Kirk Allison, 1982, 3–25, especially pp. 6ff) that all of Jesus' disciples seem to have fled earlier that day or the night before, and that it was the women who came back to the cross to watch with Jesus, while the others remained hidden. She cites several contemporary historians (Tacitus and Josephus) who write about persons standing near a cross and showing signs of grief and being killed or arrested. In staying as close to the cross as they did, the women incurred great risk.

Schottroff goes on to point out that for the women to be at

the grave of Jesus was also very dangerous. "The women wanted to anoint the corpse of Jesus with aromatic oil, they wanted to honor the dead by this, to witness their faithfulness. One must clearly understand the situation: Had they been found at the grave by denunciators, it could have cost them their lives." She cites Petronius who describes people burying a crucified victim who are caught at the tomb and crucified themselves.

5. See Leviticus 15:19–30.

6. See Luke 8:40–56; Matthew 9:18–26; Mark 5:21–34.

7. Jesus calls this woman back to him to speak out about what has happened to her (Luke 8:44–48). It may be that Jesus wanted to make clear to the crowds that he had touched someone who was "unclean."

8. See Luke 8:1–3. Joanna may well have been in (or at least closely associated with) Herod's court when the daughter of Herodias, Herod's wife, danced and John the Baptist was beheaded (Matthew 14:1–12). Certainly she would have come to Jesus out of that atmosphere of wealth, debauchery and lust. She may well have had more political sense than the other disciples.

9. See Matthew 13:1–9; Mark 4:1–9; Luke 8:4–8.

10. See Luke 13:10–17.

11. Mary Evans in her book *Woman in the Bible* (Downers Grove, IL: InterVarsity Press, 1983) points out that "Son of Abraham" was a common term, but "daughter of Abraham" is "virtually unknown in Judaistic writings" (46).

12. See Luke 1:26–38.

13. See Luke 2:1–20.

14. See Leviticus 12; Luke 2:22–24.

15. See Luke 2:25–35.

16. See Luke 2:36–38.

17. See Matthew 2:1–5.

18. See Luke 2:3–40.

19. See Matthew 2:16–18.

20. See Luke 8:2–3.

21. Traditionally Mary Magdalene was considered to be the same as Mary, sister of Martha who anointed Jesus at Bethany (John 12:1–11) and the sinful woman, spoken of by Luke (Luke 7:36–50), but "the gospels give no real support to either identification and they have now been abandoned by the [Roman Catholic] Church" (*Oxford Dictionary of the Christian Church*).

22. Generally, women were deemed unworthy to study the Torah. Evans points out in her *Woman in the Bible* that the Talmud suggests, "let the Torah rather be destroyed by fire than imparted to woman" and "whoever teaches his daughter Torah is as though he taught her obscenities" (qtd. 36.) Although one cannot fully assume practice from these kinds of statements, Jewish men prayed this prayer daily:

> Blessed be God that he has not made me a Gentile.
>
> Blessed be God that he has not made me a woman.
>
> Blessed be God that he has not made me a boor.

Sometimes the word "slave" was substituted for "boor." Notice the contrast between this prayer and what is thought to be part of the baptismal service in the early church: "As many of you as were baptized into Christ have clothed yourselves with Christ. There is no longer Jew or Greek, there is no longer slave or free, there is no longer male and female; for all of you are one in Christ Jesus" (Galations 3:27–28).

What does seem to be clear is that women in first-century Judaism had access to the sacred only in and through the patriarchal family: "Women are sanctified through the deeds of men" (Jacob Neusner, *Method and Meaning in Ancient Judaism,* Brown Judaic Studies 10, Missoula, MT: Scholars Press, 1979, 100).

23. Magdala is also thought to be Dalmanutha referred to in Mark 8:10.

24. See Luke 3:1–18; Matthew 3:1–12; Mark 1:1–8.

25. Luke 13:20–21; Matthew 13:44–46; Luke 15:8–10.

26. Luke 6:20–36; Matthew 5:2–48.

27. Matthew 9:32–34.

28. See Luke 11:14–23. There were Jewish healers and exorcists, but

the exorcisms were seldom successful and were accompanied by long and complicated rites. See Acts 19:13–17.

29. When Jesus taught that for a man to lust after a woman was sin, this was a tremendous shock to his male listeners—they were just doing what came naturally, but was women's fault. See Matthew 5:27–28. In fact, according to the law at the time, a woman couldn't prosecute her husband for infidelity; "adultery was (in the eyes of the law) possible only for a man with a married woman" (Everett Ferguson, *Backgrounds of Early Christianity,* Grand Rapids, MI: Eerdmans, 1987, 57), a crime against her husband, a violation of his property. Similarly when Jesus taught that men could not divorce at will, it would have been shocking to his listeners, because men had had the freedom to hand a woman a divorce paper and be free. See Dt. 24:1–4; Matthew 5:31–32; Matthew 19:3–9; Mark 10:2–12.

30. See Luke 8:3.

31. See Luke 7:36–50.

32. Church historian H. C. Frend says this of Jesus' attitude toward women: "Indeed, his attitude towards women was revolutionary, and may have contributed to his final break with the Pharisees" (*The Rise of Christianity,* Philadelphia; Fortress, 1984, 67). Frend sees Jesus' response to this woman's anointing him as one of the key moments in his ministry. In an era when it was taboo to speak to one's wife in public, let alone another woman (see Evans, 35, or Swidler, 187), Jesus' affirmation of this sinful woman—allowing her to touch him and speaking to her—was shocking in a way that we can hardly imagine. H. C. Frend goes on to observe, "The rebuke to Simon the Pharisee (Luke 7:39–50) was severe and it was combined with an assertion of personal authority. 'Therefore I tell you, her sins, which are many, are forgiven, for she loved much; but he who is forgiven little, loves little' (Luke 7:47). It is difficult to see how the Pharisees could have done other than oppose Jesus after this" (67).

33. See Luke 10:38–42.

34. See Luke 5:33–39; Matthew 9:14–17; Mark 2:18–22.

35. See Luke 8:26–39.

36. See Matthew 20:20–28.

37. See Luke 4:16–30; Matthew 13:54–58; Mark 6:1–6.

38. See Luke 7:11–17. In Judaism at this time, to be a widow was a disgrace and a reproach (Isaiah 54:4). The widow at Nain, according to Swidler in *Biblical Affirmations of Women,* "was by custom thought to have caused the early death of her child (he is called 'young man' by Jesus) by her sins" (215).

39. See Luke 10:38–42.

40. In her essay "The-Human-Not-Quite-Human," Dorothy L. Sayers comments on this passage: "God, of course, may have his own opinion, but the Church is reluctant to endorse it. I think I have never heard a sermon preached on the story of Martha and Mary that did not attempt, somehow, somewhere, to explain away its text. Mary's, of course, was the better part—the Lord said so, and we must not precisely contradict Him. But we will be careful not to despise Martha. No doubt, He approved of her too. We could not get on without her, and indeed (having paid lip-service to God's opinion) we must admit that we greatly prefer her. For Martha was doing a really feminine job, whereas Mary was just behaving like any other disciple, male or female; and that is a hard pill to swallow" (46–47 in *Are Women Human?*, Grand Rapids, MI: Eerdmans, 1992).

41. See Luke 1:5–25; 39–45.

42. See Luke 3:19–20; Matthew 14:3–12.

43. See Luke 8:19–21; 11:27–28; 12:49–53; 14:26; Matthew 12:46–50; Mark 3:31–35.

44. See Luke 1:46–55.

45. See Luke 11:39–52; Matthew 23:1–36; Mark 12:38–40.

46. See Matthew 21:31. Jesus often refers to the tax collectors, sinners, and prostitutes. We must remember that this grouping "characterizes not just a morally reprehensible group of people but even more a class so destitute they must engage in 'dishonorable' professions to survive" (Elisabeth Schüssler Fiorenza, *In Memory of Her: A*

Feminist Theological Reconstruction of Christian Origins, New York: Crossroad, 1983, 127).

47. See John 8:2–11.

48. See Luke 19:29–40; Matthew 21:1–9; Mark 11:1–10.

49. See Luke 13:34–35; Matthew 23:37–39.

50. See Luke 19:45–48; Matthew 21:12–17; Mark 11:15–19.

51. See Luke 20:1–8; Matthew 21:23–27; Mark 11:27–33.

52. Luke 21:2.

53. Matthew 24:1–3; Luke 21:5–7; Mark 13:1–4.

54. Luke 23:33–49; Matthew 27:33–56; Mark 15:22–41.

55. John 11:1–44.

56. Although the Pharisees and their followers believed in a final resurrection, Martha takes the declaration further in her next statement. In her affirmation of faith, she uses exactly the same words in Greek as Peter does in his better-known confession (compare John 11:27 and Matthew 16:16). Although it is not unusual to find similar wording within the synoptic gospels, it is unusual between John and Matthew. In this gospel, the great confession of who Jesus is comes from Martha.

57. John 12:1–8.

58. Luke 24:1.

59. John 20:1, 11–16. The women would have known that the danger of going to the tomb had not lessened between Friday and Sunday. To be seen at the tomb of a crucified person, particularly one perceived as a political problem by the Romans, would have been very dangerous.

The fact that the women were going to anoint the body shows that they believed Jesus to be dead. But they defied the danger of visiting a tomb, and thus were the first to greet their resurrected teacher and friend.